Redefining your perspective
from *I quit* to *I refuse to quit*.

Though marriage can be one of the best decisions you make in life, it often starts far from the *happily ever after* seen in fairytales. However, there is great love and fulfillment with marriage between a couple committed to doing the work.

- What happens when the bliss wears off?
- What happens when proclivities and old habits keep your marriage at a standstill?
- How do you handle feeling that your marriage is in a cycle of defeat or regret?
- Did you ever think you'd wonder, *Who am I married to, and why?*

When challenges with burn out, exhaustion, and defeat replace love and romance, many throw in the towel and declare, "*I QUIT!*"

The marriage journey was just as difficult for Jonathan & Ayanna. They share their roadmap for overcoming hurt, rejection, self-sabotage, and destruction while offering tested and proven strategies that will guide your marriage. No matter the stage, all (considering marriage, engaged, newlywed, veteran couples, troubled marriages, or even good relationships) can benefit from these essential tools.

With passion and insight from the science of psychology and their faith, you will experience dual perspectives as you travel with the Kilgores. They can help you recognize areas in your life and marriage that need to be abandoned. These strategies will challenge you and create the agents of change.

Rekindle the fire, restore the love,
and reinvent your marriage,
when walking away seems the best option.
Allow your marriage to be saved!

What Readers Are Saying...

Excellent! Excellent and so desperately needed. Thank you Jonathan and Ayanna! This book is choked-full of truth and wisdom. It is a sweet and delicious recipe for a successful marriage, a healing aid to marriages that are on the brink of destruction, while at the same time it is a no-holes barred call to BOTH sides to stand up, join forces, make necessary adjustments and fight for the sanctity...the precious sacredness of marriage. No easy feat, but worth it! Oh how sweet the outcome can be. So much better than ever imagined. I have been married for over 30 years and I was able to glean countless golden nuggets that I can and will use in my own marriage. I was reminded how easy it is to fall into routines so that we stop nurturing the love and commitment. No more! Also wanted to say that this book is a wonderful gift to give to engaged couples, newly weds and those that have been married for a long time as well!!!

Karen Abercrombie,
Award winning actress, film producer, writer

Oh man. So much of this is similar because I experienced quite a bit of trauma so I relate to you so much! Authenticity and transparency mean so much to me. Thank you so much for sharing your story because I know it's going to help me in this season!

Christy Freeland,
Owner at *7 Endeavors Consulting, LLC*

The concept in your writing is really strong. I absolutely love your honesty, conversational quality, and humor as you give great descriptions! You are taking the reader on a journey, and incorporating Scripture into it is fantastic! It's beautiful.

Felicity Fox
Managing Editor, ethos collective

The stories you shared were relatable and honest, something that I think many people are afraid to be anymore.

Jill Ellis,
Founder, The Pneuma Project

What a great premise for a book this was. I found your format compelling and relatable. I feel this book could have a positive impact on so many people who may be struggling to find balance and meaning in their own marriages.

Denise Mastrocola

I
QUIT

Proven Strategies to Rekindle, Restore, and Reinvent
Your Marriage When Walking Away Seems Right

I
QUIT

Proven Strategies to Rekindle, Restore, and Reinvent Your Marriage When Walking Away Seems Right

JONATHAN & AYANNA KILGORE

                    ⌐AAE

Published by Author Academy Elite
PO Box 43, Powell, OH 43065
www.AuthorAcademyElite.com

Library of Congress Control Number: 2020923627

ISBN: 978-1-64746-637-4 (paperback)
ISBN: 978-1-64746-638-1 (hardback)
ISBN: 978-1-64746-639-8 (ebook)

Available in paperback, hardback, e-book, and audiobook

Unless otherwise indicated, all Scripture quotations are from The ESV® Bible (The Holy Bible, English Standard Version®), copyright © 2001 by Crossway, a publishing ministry of Good News Publishers. Used by permission. All rights reserved.

Scripture quotations marked (AMP) are taken from the Amplified Bible, Copyright © 2015 by The Lockman Foundation. Used by permission.

Scripture quotations marked NLT are taken from the Holy Bible, *New Living Translation*, copyright 1996, 2004. Used by permission of Tyndale House Publishers, Inc., Wheaton, Illinois 60189. All rights reserved.

Scripture quotations marked (NIV) are taken from the Holy Bible, New International Version®, NIV®. Copyright © 1973, 1978, 1984, 2011 by Biblica, Inc.® Used by permission of Zondervan. All rights reserved worldwide. www.zondervan.com The "NIV" and "New International Version" are trademarks registered in the United States Patent and Trademark Office by Biblica, Inc.®

Scriptures marked as "(GNT)" are taken from the **Good News Translation - Second Edition** © 1992 by American Bible Society. Used by permission.

The KJV is public domain in the United States.

Dedication

To Grandma Turner (Ayanna's maternal grandmother).

Our grandmother was the reason we made it through our first years of marriage. She unbiasedly taught us how to love each other and stick together in the good and bad seasons. She taught us how to stick it out by putting—and keeping—God first. She chastened when necessary and gave advice along with scripture to guide us.

Thank you, Grandma, for praying with us and being an example of a godly, submitted, and prayerful wife. We love and miss you, —Jonathan & Yanna

CONTENTS

A LETTER TO YOU-THE READER   XIII

OUR STORY   XVII

LADIES FIRST

I QUIT LOVING HIM MY WAY   3

I QUIT LOVING HIM THROUGH MY REJECTION   11

I QUIT LIVING BEHIND THE GATES   19

I QUIT PLAYING THE BLAME GAME   29

I QUIT THINKING IT WAS ALL ABOUT ME   35

I QUIT LOVING HIM BY DEFINITION ONLY   45

(FLIP THE BOOK)

GENTLEMEN NEXT

I QUIT COMPLAINING	59
I QUIT CONTROLLING MY MARRIAGE	69
I QUIT LIVING IN THE PAST	81
I QUIT TRYING TO BE THE PROVIDER	87
I QUIT BEING "BUSY" AND STARTED PAYING ATTENTION	95
I QUIT COACHING AND STARTED HAVING CONVERSATIONS	103
I QUIT TAKING LIFE FOR GRANTED	109

TOGETHER AT LAST

THEOLOGY OF MARRIAGE	117
WE QUIT USING THE "D" WORD	123
WE MEET IN THE MIDDLE	131

APPENDECIES

NOTES

ACKNOWLEDGEMENTS

ABOUT THE AUTHORS

EVALUATE YOUR MARRIAGE

YOUR NEXT BEST STEPS

A LETTER TO YOU-
THE READER

As you begin to use this tool, it is our hope you hear your story within our words. We hope you use our words to get yourself to a new place of happiness in your marriage. You may find your story is exactly like what we experienced in our marriage, or you may find our experiences to be slightly or entirely different. Perhaps you are an engaged couple planning to get married and want to know how to keep the great things you have in your current relationship, or you may be newlyweds who want to know how to avoid some pitfalls. Maybe you have been married only a few years and are starting to feel some strain on your marriage, or perhaps you are a veteran who is about to throw in the towel. You may even be happily married and simply want it to stay that way. Whatever the case, it is our hope that our journey motivates you to look deeper into your own and find what you need to quit in order to save your marriage and make it better.

Are you at a point where you feel like enough is enough? Have you ever found yourself looking at your spouse and asking yourself, "Who did I marry and why?" We wrote this book for married couples who may be facing the challenges of burnout, exhaustion, or possibly even being on the verge of giving up. In this book, you will find tested strategies that we used to actually save our marriage and restore our relationship, which caused us to experience real love exactly as we dreamed it could be. We have also recommended these strategies to the countless numbers of couples we have mentored and coached into healthier, happier, and better marriage relationships.

You may find yourself thinking, "But my spouse won't read this. They're not interested." That's okay too! You only need to work on yourself at this point. This is not an opportunity to place blame and find all the ways your spouse needs to change. Rather, this is a personal assessment and evaluation of what you need to quit doing and what you are willing to admit and alleviate in order to make your marriage relationship better. The first step to making your marriage better is realizing you have to put in the initial work to improve yourself. Make a conscious decision that you are going to focus on what you need to do and not what your spouse is or is *not* doing. As they see a change in you, you will likely begin to see a change in them. Don't wait—start with yourself. *Start now!*

The act of quitting actually requires you to make a choice. Choose to quit placing blame. Choose to take responsibility. This book will help you see areas in your life and marriage that need quitting. It will illuminate proclivities and patterns keeping your marriage in a holding pattern or at a standstill. If you feel like your marriage is in a cycle of defeat, regret, or disappointment, this is the road map for you. When properly followed, it will not only cause personal change by encouraging you to refocus and redefine your role in the marriage, but it will revive and reignite the passion you have for each other. It will guide you down a path toward reinventing your marriage to be healthy, happy, sustainable, lasting, and whole.

How to read this book

Continue reading this side of the book to read Ayanna's perspective and the things she quit first. When you complete this side, flip the book and continue reading from the back to read Jonathan's perspective and how we got on the same page.

You will find reflection questions at the end of each chapter. Printable downloads are available on the resources page at www.Vow2Cherish.com for your convenience.

When you get to the end of the book, let us hear about your journey! Did our journey mirror any portion of your marriage journey or did it differ? How?

Be sure to write a review on Amazon and like us on Facebook @Vow2Cherish and follow us on Instagram @Vow2Cherish. Send us a direct message or inbox message. Don't have social media? Shoot us an email at info@vow2cherish.com.

We would love to be a part of your next marriage event and to have you join us for our next challenge, meet-up, date-night, or marriage event. Visit us at www.vow2cherish.com for more information on how to make that happen!

—Jonathan & Ayanna

OUR STORY

Hi, I'm Ayanna, and our story began when we were mere babes. It was the summer before my fourteenth birthday—June 19, 1989, to be exact. I was thirteen, and Jonathan was fourteen. I was invited to an overnight youth camp at a church I had never even visited before. I remember the first day. We arrived early and met the camp director and her son, but it wasn't long before others began to arrive. I remember being so nervous and shy because I didn't know anyone there except my brother.

The night went on, and more children and teenagers arrived. Everyone seemed pretty nice. We were meeting new people, and it looked as though the week wasn't going to be so bad after all. There were many parents dropping off their kids. Some were with siblings, others with their church groups, and some seemed to be alone. It wasn't long before I knew who I would be sharing a room with. As the sanctuary filled up, another family came in that included a teenage boy, a girl, an adult guy, and a very tall older gentleman. I can remember thinking, "Wow, that man is tall and looks so mean."

The next day, word got to me that Jonathan liked me. I wasn't even sure who Jonathan was. However, it was soon brought to my attention that he had come with the tall man's family the night before. He was the youngest son.

I remember our first interaction that week. A water balloon fight had broken out at camp. Somehow, he managed to bust a water balloon on me, and I vowed to get him back. I am not sure if I ever got him back or not, but I do remember it was a very fun week filled with classes, church services, teen talks, kickball, and roller skating.

One night, while I was talking with some of the girls, someone threw a note from the boys' floor up to our window. It was from Jonathan to me, and it read, "Will you go with me?" There were three boxes—*yes*, *no*, and *maybe*—and I had to choose one. I didn't respond but told him I'd let him know my answer the next day. Well, as you can guess, I checked the *yes* box, and our journey began. We endured a long-distance relationship throughout high school and most of college with a few interruptions, but we always managed to find our way back to each other.

On June 12, 1996, the summer before my senior year of college, we eloped. We went to the courthouse with a few of my close friends. I was twenty, and Jon was twenty-one; we were both still in college. Yet there I stood, preparing for a lifetime commitment, in many ways still a little girl. We kept our marriage secret for nearly a year, not even telling our parents until my graduation in March of the following year. That's when Jonathan left his parents' home and moved to my college town where we found a small, inexpensive two-bedroom apartment. We immediately began planning a public wedding for two months later in May 1997. Little did we know within those two months I would become pregnant with our oldest child. So, although we were married and had been married for nearly a year, we had not even lived together for a good two months before we had to start thinking about ourselves as a family of three.

On May 17, 1997, wedding bells rang (for a second time). We were publicly wed before hundreds of family members and friends, and we began a very modest married life. It was the start of what we thought would be our happily ever after. Jonathan was working as a traveling life insurance agent, and I got a job as a kindergarten teacher right out of college. We were still babies, only twenty-one and twenty years old, now married and about to have a baby of our own in a few short months while still trying to learn how to be married and live with each other. Our pastor at the time refused to give us marital counseling because we were, as he saw it, already married and didn't need it. We depended on what we thought we knew and what we could figure out. Quite frankly, we were still learning how to be adults.

We would continue to grow in our relationship, facing each obstacle as it came. Some we tackled, others we jumped over, and the rest beat us down. We would have two more children within our first six years of marriage. We had gotten to the point where we were tired of being married, tired of trying to make it work, and tired of our marriage feeling like a failure. We were ready to throw in the towel and call it quits.

I felt like something was always missing in our marriage. I wrote a list of reasons to quit with most of the reasons on my list pointing to the faults and shortcomings of my husband. We had tried and tried on our own. We made attempts with professional and even pastoral counseling. No matter how much we did or what we tried, it felt like we simply didn't click anymore. Challenges from the early stages of our marriage and the complexity of a long-term relationship that had lost its sizzle stared us in the face. It was at this moment God downloaded strategies for us to use to save our marriage. We had to *quit*, but we didn't need to quit the marriage, and we didn't need to quit each other. We needed to quit the destructive habits that were sabotaging our marriage. Quitting saved our marriage!

We had to change our perspective to understand how quitting isn't always a bad thing. When we'd reached the place where I wanted to quit on my marriage, quit trying to make it work, and quit trying to be a couple, I realized that even though it had been nearly twenty years, I had not yet tried everything. There were ways to make my marriage better, to make it what I wanted it to be, to make it work. So, by not making another attempt, I would do more than quit on my marriage and my family. I would fail it. If you have not tried everything to make something work and you still walk away from it, you aren't simply quitting. You are choosing to fail. However, it is acceptable to quit the right things for the right reasons if you want to see real change.

God gave me a list of things I had to *quit* first before I could quit being married. He wasn't going to allow me to simply take an F. I had to give it my best shot. Then, if it still didn't work, at least I'd given the effort. I had to take a long look at myself and my ways and realize I wasn't married to myself. Jonathan wasn't going to do things the way I did or say things the way I said them. I needed to take a hard look at what I needed to change in order to stay married to my husband.

We have a grace story. What happened to us may not be uncommon, but it was a miracle. And we realized someone needed the story of our miracle. The easy thing to do was go through what we went through and walk in the victory of it leaving it there. (That's what I wanted to do.) After all, most don't know the details of what we went through, so why even bring it up? However, that is not why God allowed us to live through our experience. The victory of what we went through came with a responsibility to share with others. Somebody needs to hear our experience so they, too, can know how they can experience the same thing (or something similar) and get through it victoriously. There are couples who need to know they are not the only ones going through what they are facing. Other couples have experienced the same thing, and some are experiencing it now.

We have all experienced failure and defeat in our marriages, but we have also experienced victory and triumph. Hang in there! Keep pushing! Keep praying! Keep showing up! Marriage is a beautiful thing, but it's not an easy breeze. It takes hard work. It takes commitment. It takes the decision to be intentional, and it takes real team effort.

We decided it would be heartbreaking to God if we got through all we did and then on the other side pretended we were alright and had no turmoil or challenges. We couldn't stand before couples and tell them to do this or work on that without being authentic and honest. Although we make no claims for guaranteed success, we want you to know that we know you can do this when we are recommending you try this or that because it is what we did when we were in your shoes.

We don't want to tell you only how we made it through the financial struggles. We don't want to simply tell you about the challenges we came through with our children at different ages and stages. We want to tell you something real. If we are going to kill the force tearing marriages and relationships apart, we have to have couples who are willing to stand up and be real and honest and lay it out there as it is, even the ugly parts. We have seen enough fake marriages! Those who live one way in public and another way behind closed doors. We know there are real deals out here making it work. *Day—by—day!*

LADIES FIRST

AYANNA'S PERSPECTIVE

1993

1997

I QUIT LOVING
HIM MY WAY

"Better communication between couples can be accomplished when one can demonstrate caring to the other person in a language the recipient understands."

—Gary Chapman

We often love the way we need to be loved. However, according to Gary Chapman[1], relationships grow better when we understand each other. Everyone gives and receives love differently, but with a little insight into these differences, we can be confidently equipped to communicate love well. In order for your spouse to feel loved, you must express your love to them, but you cannot adequately express or communicate love to your spouse unless you know and speak their love language.

Learning a different language can be very difficult. It takes time and requires lots of practice and study. I can remember taking French as a ninth-grade student in high school. The first semester that I took French I had Madame Sophia. She was a native of France and spoke French fluently. As a matter of fact, French was her first language. Though her class was quite a challenge, I earned an A. I learned the ins and outs of the language, the grammar, and the culture. It was quite an experience. However, I heard from other students that the other French teacher, Mrs. Richardson, was a lot easier than Mme Sophia. So, the next year I took Mrs. Richardson's class. Mrs. Richardson was from the United States and had grown up in South Georgia. She had a thick Southern drawl that was very distinct, even in her delicate French vocabulary. Her *bonjour* lacked French flair and sounded like "bone-jew-er." Needless to say, although I got an A in her class, I didn't learn much. In fact, I forgot much of what I had previously learned.

For many years we hosted international exchange students in our home. We had students from China, Korea, Africa, India, Russia, and Vietnam living with us. We quickly learned how a difference in language can be a huge barrier in a relationship. Not only does it impede and damper basic communication, but it can also prevent you from bonding and connecting with the individual. There were many moments in our home when the students would hear what was said in a general conversation, but because they had little understanding of the English language, they would not respond properly and sometimes would not respond at all. If we took time to give clarity and explain the message we were trying to convey, they would eventually understand. The same is true in relationships with our spouses. We have to be able to speak their language. If we don't speak their language, the message can be lost in translation and interpretation. So, if you don't know your love language or that of your spouse, I encourage you to find out what it is.

Now, mind you: I knew my love language, and I wanted him to speak it and would get annoyed when he didn't. However, I would then turn around and make excuses as to why I couldn't and didn't speak his love language. Talk about a double standard, but it was more than that. I didn't realize how not speaking his language went deeper than me not understanding his language or simply being insensitive and selfish.

Our basic love language is the way we naturally give and receive love. However, there was a hidden, underlying factor preventing me from speaking my husband's love language. It took me years after being married and receiving some good counseling to recognize and uncover the reason.

Physical touch is one of my husband's primary languages. So, for him, holding hands, random hugs, and passionate kisses scream, *I love you!* But to me, physical touch doesn't quite express the same sentiments. Actually, those actions didn't say "I love you" to me at all. Now, don't get me wrong. I absolutely love touch. I mean, who doesn't like a gentle pat on the butt while you're cooking dinner? Or a walk up from behind while I brushed my teeth followed by a gentle hug around the waist? We are human, right? It simply didn't say "I love you" to me and definitely didn't carry the same weight for me as it did for my husband. We did all of those things—I even initiated some physical touch like cuddling and holding hands. But our interpretations were different.

I was molested in the third grade by an older teenaged cousin. No, this was not a one-time thing. It happened often over the course of a few months at least. (I was eight years old, so I don't have a full recollection of how long it was.) Actually, by definition I was raped and molested. My mom worked third shift at the hospital when I was growing up, and she and my father divorced when my siblings and I were very young. Being a single parent, she solicited the assistance of my grandmother to care for us while she was working. I would spend a lot of time with my older sister and younger brother after school and on the weekends at Grandmama's house. During this particular time, Grandmama allowed her great-nephew to move in with her. He was enrolled at the local high school, and her house became his home for a while. Grandmama had a fairly big house, and it was not unusual for us to play upstairs whenever we were not playing outside. Regrettably, my cousin's bedroom was also upstairs.

One day, this cousin asked if I wanted to play house. For a little girl, no more than eight years old, house was a common choice to play at school and home. Little did I know he was going to teach me to play house in a much different way than I had ever played house before. I often played with my brother and boy cousins when they visited. My older sister didn't play with us much, and there were five boys (and six years) between me and my first girl cousin, who lived out of state, so I was usually the mommy.

As we were playing house, my cousin told me he would be the daddy, and I, of course, had to be the mommy. He took it upon himself to teach me what mommies and daddies do in the bedroom. I was used to being the mommy, but I thought being the mommy meant I was supposed to be the one who pretended to cook all the meals and care for the children. We had never gone this far in our imagination before. We never played in the actual bed, and we definitely never touched and explored body parts. Having grown up in a single-parent home since the age of three, I didn't have much knowledge or observation of mommy and daddy's intimate behavior besides what I saw on TV. (And if you think back to the 80s versus today, that wasn't much.)

He never threatened me. I didn't feel like I was being forced or that we were doing anything wrong. I honestly felt as if I was merely playing. I didn't realize anything wrong was happening or had happened until many years later. We played house a lot during the time he was living with my grandmother. After several visits to the doctor and a few UTIs (urinary tract infections), Grandmama told me I couldn't play upstairs anymore. I didn't understand why at the time, but being the wise woman she was, I'm sure she knew something was wrong. The problem was that she never directly addressed it.

This eventually led to me interpreting physical touch not as saying "I love you" but as a signal for "what mommies and daddies are supposed to do," and that is what was imprinted into my brain as such. As a result, physical touch to me said, "I want you to do what you're supposed to do" a lot louder than "I love you." I had to unlearn the language I had been previously taught.

Unlearning the previous language came with years of me not wanting to (or even being able to) speak my husband's true love language. Touch meant something different in my vernacular. I had to relearn that part of the love language to communicate properly with my husband. I had to be able to touch him, kiss him, and cuddle with him *without* it leading to making love or having sex. Not only this, but I had to learn that it was *his* language. If it meant "I love you" to him, it didn't have to mean "I love you" to me. It didn't need to be associated with childhood memories. The language was not indicative of my interpretation or translation. It was his "I love you" language, and he needed to hear it spoken from me.

I had to be willing to look within myself for answers to the tough question why is it so hard for me to show him the love he both needs and deserves. There were many days that I would sit and cry because part of me would want to touch him but then a part of me would be resistant. It took years to uncover the root because it had been buried so deep. But once I found it, I dug it up and destroyed it making sure it would sure it would never cause problems in this area of my marriage. I was intentional to make sure my husband heard, "I love you" through my actions as much as he heard it through my words.

As previously mentioned, he had to help me learn his language. Much as my French teachers taught me French in high school or as we taught English to our exchange students, he understood and was patient with me while I studied and practiced this new language. As an eight-year-old girl, it meant something different than it did now as an adult wife. At eight I was doing what I was told I was supposed to do. It couldn't be used in our marriage relationship to mean the same thing. Having this conversation with my husband was difficult, but it was liberating to finally understand what was frustrating both of us. We were saying the same thing in different ways, so it was translating differently to each of us because our languages were different. Jonathan and I had to work together to intentionally reprogram that language into my psyche. We had to talk about it and establish a language we both understood. We had to understand how touch does not automatically mean "it's time." I began to find security in his touch, his hug, his cuddle, and I began to speak the language he needed to hear.

YOUR TURN

Do you and your spouse know your love language?   Yes ☐   No ☐

(If no, visit https://www.5lovelanguages.com and take the assessment today.)

What are your top three primary love languages?

_____

_____

_____

What are your spouse's top three primary love languages?

_____

_____

_____

Is there anything preventing you from loving your spouse the way they desire to be?

Yes ☐   No ☐

If yes, what is it and what can you do to change it?

_____

_____

_____

Name five ways you can speak your spouse's love language?

_____

_____

_____

_____

_____

I QUIT LOVING HIM THROUGH MY REJECTION

"I feel that rejecting rejection is one of the most crucial steps in getting past failure."

—John Rampton

Some might say I was too young to experience heartbreak or even to know what it was, but I would beg to differ. Not only did I experience heartbreak, but my heartbreak quickly morphed into rejection. Honestly, the entire relationship had been birthed out of feelings of rejection, which traced back to when I was three years old and my father abandoned our family. He didn't simply divorce my mother; he abandoned us. He left without a trace, or so it seemed in my three-year-old eyes. Throughout my childhood I dealt with cycles of promises and heartbreaks from my father. This led to a life of rejection and a need for perfection.

Jonathan was my high school sweetheart. Having met him the summer before my freshman year, we practically grew up together. I thought he was cute—a little bit dorky, but cute nonetheless. Then there was me: super skinny with a Jheri curl and fresh L.A. gear high-top tennis shoes, and a long blue jean skirt. (We weren't allowed to wear pants.) There wasn't much to our relationship in the beginning. We were young, and neither of us owned a car, so our relationship consisted of phone conversations and occasional meetups once or twice a year until I got my license. After that, all bets were off. I would borrow cars from family, rent cars, get rides—whatever I had to do to see him. He would do the same and would even catch the Greyhound bus to come and see me. Once I got my own car, we would go to football games, movies, concerts, museums, and every fine dining restaurant in our city. And, of course, we went to church.

We had the typical (or not) "on again, off again" relationship many teenagers have. Although that hurt, the major heartbreak came the summer before my junior year of college. I don't even remember the reason he gave me for ending our relationship, and honestly, I don't think there ever was a real reason given. He simply cut me off.

Because I had given so much to Jonathan materially, I had very unhealthy emotional ties to him that were hard to break. I remember being so depressed. I went from being an honor roll student to getting C's and D's in all of my classes. I went on shopping binges to try to ease the pain. The worst part of it all was having to see him every Sunday because we went to the same church. I was confused. I thought he was the one and that we would be together forever. I thought we were happy. Clearly, that feeling wasn't mutual. One day I finally got the truth, the reason he broke up with me. Here's what happened:

Jonathan had been invited to a music conference in the Midwest. I helped him get his plane ticket and business cards, fund his preparations, revamp his wardrobe—the whole nine yards. By *help*, I mean I paid for it. When he left, he was really excited, but he came back a different person. I eventually found out he had developed feelings for his friend's sister while out west at the conference, and he decided she was what he wanted. He stayed with this friend and went on a couple of dates with his sister. He didn't have the nerve to immediately tell me what had actually happened, so he distanced himself from me instead. His only explanation was, "I just don't think this is going to work." I heard those words over the phone, and I instantly lost myself emotionally.

I had to work out my healing with him constantly in my face. There was no running away, and there was no hiding from him. It wasn't every day, but on Sundays we went to his dad's church, which was two hours away from my home. I rode with his family every week unless I was away at school. It was like trying to detox while still eating toxic foods.

After spending days in bed, depressed and sad, I finally prayed and asked God for answers. Why was this happening? I remember God telling me I had put Jonathan in the place where only He (God) should have been. God told me He wanted me to use this time to put Him back in the place where He belonged in my life. He clearly spoke to my heart and told me what I was experiencing was temporary. I opened my Bible and literally landed on 2 Corinthians 4:18 (AMP), which reads, "So we look not at the things which are seen, but at the things which are unseen; for the things which are visible are temporal [just brief and fleeting], but the things which are invisible are everlasting and imperishable." I remember going to a revival later that week. When I got there, the title of the woman's sermon was "It's Only Temporary." My answer was confirmed and clear, and so were my instructions.

I chose to stop focusing on the hurt and decided to concentrate on detoxing myself from the negativity of that relationship instead. I started dealing with the root of the problem that was causing me to have such unhealthy ties with him to begin with. I was always the savior in our relationship. I was always funding things, always going above and beyond, and always sacrificing. I was the one risking it all while he reaped the benefits. I took time to focus on myself, the hurts of my heart, and the Lord. When our relationship came to a halt, I regretted everything I had put into it that had not been reciprocated. I regretted buying designer jewelry and clothes and paying for dates. Though I loved him, it had not been a healthy balance. The hurt I felt caused me to shut down the giving nature of my heart, punishing others who had done nothing to deserve it. I chose to deal with it all—no matter how painful.

We had been separated for almost a year when I finally found my groove. We were still at the same church, but now I was able to come to church, serve, do what I needed to do, and then leave. I'd finally gotten my bearings when he decided he wanted to try to get my attention again. He purposely flashed his other relationships in my face to make me jealous, but I was not fazed.

Somehow or other, we ended up back together. Within six months of being reunited, we were married.

Unfortunately, I got married with a half-healed heart taking the leftover pain into my marriage with me. I hid behind the wall of distrust that was still hindering our marriage. It took years before I allowed the Holy Spirit to show me what was happening. He had to show me how I was operating and loving out of my fear of being hurt again.

I wanted my husband to love the parts of me I believed he was supposed to cover. I wanted him to fill the areas my father had left open and void. Roots of rejection and abandonment had been birthed from not having my father present for most of my life. When a young girl is growing up, daddy is her first love. Whether he is lovable or not, whether he is there or not doesn't change the fact that he is her first love. Whatever shape their relationship takes—whether or not she can rely upon him, trust him, or depend upon him—it will become either a met or an unmet need. If it becomes an unmet need, then it's often played out in the girl's marriage. Those unmet needs can get transferred to the husband because dad didn't validate her. That was the pattern I fell into with my husband, and similar things will happen with a male child if a mother doesn't validate her young boy by her words and actions, telling him, "I have time for you, you're wonderful, you are strong, I have time to listen to you." He will look for a person of the opposite gender to validate him emotionally within the context of their relationship. However, this chapter is about my rejection, not his.

Not only did I expect him to fix the rejection from my father, but I wanted him to go back and mend the wounds young Jonathan had left open. The fruits of my father's rejection did not wait until our marriage to surface but became evident even while we were dating. Instead of Jonathan meeting those needs in our dating relationship, however, he created new and deeper hurt and rejection. I in turn had to rely on God to heal those hurts instead. Once I allowed God to heal my heart, it healed my relationship with my husband. I had to quit harboring negative emotions about past incidents and situations. It was actually those harbored emotions that would surface in response to new and (most of the time) irrelevant situations. In simple terms, I had to *forgive*! I had to stop holding him captive to his own broken, hurt, unhealed, younger self. I went back and forgave him for what happened all those years ago and let him know how he actually hurt me. Moving on does not take the place of forgiveness. If you don't forgive, the hurt will stay in your heart, and you will move on while carrying all of that baggage with you. Once I did this, once I let go of it all, we were able to flourish into a healthy and happy marriage. Choosing to be healed instead of holding onto what hurt me changed the course of my marriage and my family. Today, I can truly say, "I am healed, happy, and whole."

YOUR TURN

Do you currently, or have your ever had anything in your heart against your spouse?

Yes ☐   No ☐

Can you identify the root cause of any rejection that has been present in your marriage/relationship?

_____

_____

_____

Is anything causing you to hold your spouse to unhealthy expectations (rejection, unhealed hurts, unresolved issues, etc)? If so, what?

_____

_____

_____

I QUIT LIVING
BEHIND THE GATES

"Trust in the LORD with all of your heart, and do not lean on your own understanding."

—Proverbs 3:5 (ESV)

For a season in our marriage, we lived in a "high-profile" gated community. I'm not talking about gates where you have to have a code that you can give to anyone, allowing them access. I am not talking about gates that never work and end up staying open, allowing access to anyone who desires it. These were gates with twenty-four-hour human attendants. Gates where they check your ID and call the residence you wish to visit in order to grant permission for access. Of course, as a resident you can enter guests' names via the computer or app and even may have permanent passes issued to guests upon request. Bottom line, if as a resident I didn't want to grant access to someone, I clearly didn't have to. I was safe behind the gate. As a resident I controlled who could enter my community. There was no such thing as friends or family simply being "in the neighborhood." There were no unannounced visitors, and I absolutely loved it.

Sadly, I was not only living behind a physical gate. For years in my marriage, I lived behind an emotional gate. This gate, like the physical gate to my community, had a twenty-four-hour attendant: me. I had grown accustomed to always having my guard up. My heart had been hurt previously in our marriage and our dating relationship, and I refused to be hurt again. My heart had been hurt by my father. My heart had been hurt by people in the church. My heart had been hurt by family members, and to be honest, my heart had been hurt by me. So, out of the fear of being hurt again, I put up a very high, thick, cold stone wall. What caused the wall to be so high? What architectural strategy laid the wall so thick? And why was it so very cold?

Now of course, as you can imagine, other people can hurt your heart in many different ways. Each time this happened, every time someone did something that hurt or damaged my heart, another beam was added to my wall. However, you may be wondering, "How did you hurt your own heart?" Well, I hurt my own heart and didn't even realize it until much later in my marriage. I hurt my own heart by refusing to put up boundaries and not sticking up for myself. I allowed others to continue to do things that were harming me emotionally. Some of this was out of the fear of losing a relationship or the fear of being disrespectful, and some was out of my own rejection and desire to be loved and accepted. It got to a point where I could not blame others for my hurt any longer. I had to take responsibility for it myself. I had to take full responsibility for not setting boundaries and confronting the problems and issues.

My solution? Well, I built the wall! A tall, thick, and cold wall. I would never again be hurt by others. If no one else cared enough to protect Yanna's heart, Yanna did. And boy, the wall of protection I built. To be completely honest with you, I did not stop with the wall. I had to make sure my heart would be forever protected. So, I put a gate up around the wall. This gate was an electric, high voltage gate. If anybody tried to climb it, they would be shocked down and would not succeed. I also dug a moat around this wall like the ones they describe in books. I filled the moat with piranhas. I had gone from being too open and vulnerable to literally keeping my heart so guarded it was difficult for love to come in and equally as difficult for love to go out. I moved my heart behind the gate, and I became the sole gate attendant. I made the decision of who was granted entry to my heart and exactly how much access they gained with that entry. I know it sounds pretty extreme now, but it seemed so necessary then.

Clearly, I had endured multiple occurrences of trauma. Many may wonder, what trauma have you possibly endured? Well, you have to have a clear understanding of what trauma actually is to see what I'm talking about. When my eighteen-year-old boyfriend chose to cheat on me and I found out, that was trauma. When my father walked out on my mother, sister, brother, and me—trauma. When I grew up in a single-parent home, enduring hardship, that was trauma. When I trusted people with vulnerable and confidential information that was, in turn, shared or abused—trauma. When a trusted relationship failed because of a lack of communication or miscommunication, that was trauma too. When someone is yelling at you or bullying you, that is trauma. I'm not talking about physical trauma, which may be connected to a physical injury, but emotional trauma. According to Webster, trauma is a deeply distressing (causing anxiety, sorrow, or pain) or disturbing experience; the emotional shock or response follows a stressful event. Trauma is subjective, which simply means what was traumatic for me may not be for you and vice versa.

Even though the event that caused the trauma is over, the shadow or residue from that trauma remains in the brain. You have to intentionally clean your brain pathways to clear yourself of it. I'll use the analogy of a toilet. (Stay with me—I promise when I'm finished it will make sense.) You push the button, it flushes, and everything that was collected in the bowl disappears. The bowl refills with fresh water, and it appears to be clean. However, we all know you can flush and flush and flush a toilet, refilling it with fresh water, but if you don't use a brush and toilet bowl cleaner every now and then and physically clean the bowl, residue will build up. Although you've flushed it after using it, you still have to go further and clean out the residue. Don't believe me? Only flush your toilet as a means of "cleaning" it for thirty days. With every flush, a little residue will remain. You will soon see a ring of residue building around the inner part of the bowl.

A similar thing happens in our brains after we experience stressful and emotional events if we choose to only flush them out, deal with them on the surface, or ignore them entirely. If we are not careful and intentional, a little residue will remain in the neuropathways of our brain. Such trauma can cause changes in the ventromedial prefrontal cortex region of the brain. (That's the part of the brain that regulates emotional responses.) Sweeping things under the carpet doesn't solve problems, and they won't stay there. They will resurface and cause problems in your future and your now.

Like the solid waste, the contents may be gone from the toilet, and what happened to you may be over. You may have chosen to forgive and move on, but forgiveness is more than simply saying, "Oh, I forgive them." Moving on is more than merely saying, "I'm over that." If you did not properly process the event, or if that event has occurred several times in the same or similar way, then your body, brain, hormones, and molecular structure will hold onto the effects the event had on you. The memory of the event and the emotions associated with the event live in your body and are stored in your brain, even though you may try to push them out of your subconscious.

If you are not careful, you will be safe, but your body will be in the habit of expecting the trauma based on what you have experienced. Our bodies often respond to what our brain has forgotten or suppressed. Fear and anxiety are often triggered by familiar and even unfamiliar stimuli. Have you ever smelled a fragrance that reminded you of something from your past, maybe your childhood or a past relationship? I remember a few years after my grandmother passed away, I walked past someone in the mall who was wearing the perfume fragrance she always wore (Estee Lauder). Without even thinking about it, I immediately burst into tears and began to miss her. My brain at the time was not thinking about her, but when the smell reached my nose, it immediately connected to my ventromedial prefrontal cortex(the part of the brain that processes fear and causes emotional responses). The emotional response was tears. Though that was a good memory, there have been times when the memories weren't so good. It's how our bodies are wired, but when it comes to trauma, the response or memory may not be a pleasant one. Maybe your husband grabbed your arm a certain way or said the wrong thing. If it's a suppressed memory or situation you have buried, you may respond and not understand why you are reacting or responding the way you are. You may be responded to the memory that was triggered and not the what's actually happening.

Did you know you can live with a foreign object in your body for so long that it actually becomes a part of you and you don't even notice it anymore? Through calcification, the body will cover the foreign object, and it will camouflage the object into the tissues. Since you somehow ignored all the alarms, signals, and warnings your brain sent out to the different parts of your body, it will in time say internally, "Okay, I guess this is how it's supposed to be," and it will stop sending the warning signals. Have you ever gotten into a car and forgotten to put on your seatbelt? The red bell will flash, and the alarm will sound for quite a while. I have on occasion ignored the alarm and the flash, as annoying as it was, long enough that it eventually stopped. No, I didn't put my seat belt on. And yes, for a while after the audible alarm sounded, the visual alarm flashed on my dashboard. But again, after a significant amount of time and without putting on my seatbelt, the alarms stopped completely.

The same happens in our brain, and that's where I had gotten with my heart, not only in my relationship with my husband but in all relationships. I would love only so deep. I would let a select few in, but only so far. I would only trust people with so much. To guard myself against the possible hurt that might come later, I decided I had to be careful of what was allowed in my life. I was so on guard that I stifled and sabotaged genuine relationships. Sadly, I didn't see anything wrong with it. I saw and accepted it as "the way I was." Though it was the way I had become and *seemed* to be the way I had always been, it was not the way I had been created nor the way I needed to be.

I had to learn to trust again. And in actuality I had to learn to trust God again. I have a gift of faith, so I can and do believe in God's love and care. However, I didn't trust Him with my heart issues. He was my source; He would always provide and even heal. I could believe God would heal you and everybody else, but I never had faith He would heal my heart. Honestly, I never actually asked for healing because I didn't even realize it was a problem. I didn't recognize my own heart issue, didn't realize my own need for inner healing. It was how I was, it had become a part of me, and I had learned to live with it. I had to allow God to let the drawbridge down. I couldn't trust him (my husband) and them (other people) until I fully trusted *Him* (Abba Father, God). Once I let *Him* do for me what no one else could do, once I let *Him* clean out all the mistrust and debris and residue, and once I accepted help from a professional counselor, then I was able to let the necessary people in. I was able to recognize and release unhealthy relationships that had caused me to retreat behind the wall.

I was ready to impart the love necessary for the people in my life. I was able to love my husband the way he needed to be loved. I was able to love my children and family the way they needed to be loved. I was free to be myself, a true and authentic *me*. I was no longer the me I had grown accustomed to, the me I had lived with for years. I was at last the me that had been hidden under years of betrayal, hurt, misuse, abuse, misunderstanding, unappreciation, rejection, and abandonment.

I had to be healed. You have to be healed. Therapy, counseling, coaching, or deliverance—whatever healing looks like for you will start the process. Unpack what has been buried or put away. It's the easiest way to avoid cycles of negative reactivity and shame. Get back to your real and authentic *you*. Let the drawbridge down and open the gates!

YOUR TURN

What unresolved issues have you learned to live with in your marriage/relationship?

_____

_____

_____

What prevents you from being truly vulnerable with your spouse in all areas?

_____

_____

_____

I QUIT PLAYING THE BLAME GAME

"A snowflake is one of God's most fragile creations but look what they can do when they stick together!"

– Author Unknown

One of the biggest cycles we get caught by in a marriage (or any relationship for that matter) is the blame game. More often than not, the blamer does not take the blame but instead places it on another: a spouse, children, their job, their past, or any source other than themselves. How far back does this blame game go? We can look back as far as Adam and Eve, the first example we have of marriage on Earth. The Bible says that as soon as Adam and Eve ate the fruit of the tree, their eyes were opened, and they realized they were naked:

And they heard the sound of the Lord God walking in the garden in the cool [afternoon breeze] of the day, so the man and his wife hid and kept themselves hidden from the [d]presence of the Lord God among the trees of the garden. But the Lord God called to Adam, and said to him, "Where are you?" He said, "I heard the sound of You [walking] in the garden, and I was afraid because I was naked; so, I hid myself." God said, "Who told you that you were naked? Have you eaten [fruit] from the tree of which I commanded you not to eat?"

—Genesis 3:8-11(ESV)

Instead of taking responsibility for his actions and behavior and answering God's question, Adam placed blame and responded to the question through deflection. "And the man said, 'The woman whom You gave to be with me—she gave me [fruit] from the tree, and I ate it.'" (Genesis 3:12 AMP). Adam blamed Eve, the woman God gave him, and then blamed God for giving him the woman. So, God then questioned her: "Then the Lord God said to the woman, 'What is this that you have done?' The woman said, 'The serpent beguiled *and* deceived me, and I ate [from the forbidden tree]'" (Genesis 3:13 AMP). Eve was stating a fact; she had been deceived by the serpent. However, the truth is she was blaming the devil because she didn't want to take full responsibility for her actions either.

Quitting the act of placing blame means you choose to take responsibility because you know what you did. Taking responsibility and owning up to your actions is very important and vital for a healthy relationship. It not only gives you control of your role in the relationship, but it fosters trust and dependability. Being responsible for your actions communicates to your spouse that you are willing to be honest. It shows a level of vulnerability, which is very encouraging and shows you are authentic and open. On the flip side, taking responsibility means accepting the fact that everyone makes mistakes; *you* make mistakes.

I had to realize I was not perfect. Some of my behavior was in fact unhealthy, and I had to take ownership of that unhealthy behavior. I was no different from any other human, and I, too, found ways to blame my unhappiness, my dysfunction, and even challenges in my marriage on others. Sadly, my husband got most of that blame. If we had a disagreement, I would always find a way to blame him. It was something *he* either did or didn't do, which made it all *his* fault. In my warped perspective, I was always the victim. It came to the point where I could no longer blame my dad, my mom, my sister, my brother, my family, my past, or my husband. I had to take a long look at Yanna and say, "This is what you did. This is what you said." I had absolutely no control over what anyone else did or said to me. I did, however, have control of what I did or said in response. Taking responsibility meant acknowledging and taking ownership of every single action I did and every word I said.

Taking responsibility meant being aware of defensive responses such as "You should have told me that" or "I didn't realize it was that serious to you." I had to be aware of myself. In return, my husband became more aware of himself. He started taking responsibility for his actions and words. That meant openly communicating about our feelings, desires, and needs. It meant being willing to admit we didn't have everything all together in all areas. It meant growing from the challenges in our relationship. I was owning my behavior and holding myself accountable for my actions, and my husband was doing the same.

Now, this didn't mean I took blame that wasn't mine (and vice versa). That's actually not taking responsibility. Let's not get confused—that is accepting blame that has been misplaced. I didn't automatically accept responsibility simply because my husband said something was my fault. I didn't make excuses for my husband's inexcusable behavior or my own. That is very unhealthy and can lead to accepting other unhealthy behaviors.

So, what does this look like? Well, for example, suppose I bring my husband a cheeseburger on a plate and say, "Hey, babe, I got you a burger." Then, he says, "Oh, but it has cheese on it. Why did you get cheese on it?" A defensive response from me would be to say, "Well, you should have told me you didn't like cheese. How was I supposed to know?" Why would someone respond in such a defensive way? Well, when people are held accountable for their behavior, especially their mistakes, they often respond on the defensive. They react instead of acting on the situation, and they are usually reacting to emotion more than what actually occurred. In the example, I defensively reacted to my husband being upset about the cheese. Instead of reacting, I should have acted on the need to take responsibility for my mistake. A healthy response would have been to say, "Oh, I apologize. I should have asked you what you wanted on your burger instead of assuming you wanted what I wanted. I didn't realize you didn't want cheese. That's my mistake. What can I get you instead?"

I came to the realization I had to be responsible for and take control of the mistakes I made, whether they were big or small. When both parties can actually begin to take responsibility for the situation that occurred, you can begin to rebuild trust. This can be tough, especially when you feel like you have been wronged in the situation. You may feel as though you are the victim. However, taking responsibility is necessary if you want to restore trust and save your relationship/marriage. What did you do to contribute to this happening? I'm not saying you are the one to blame or that it was your fault, but what was your contribution? Most of the time there is mutual responsibility to be shared.

Let me be honest. This was not an easy habit to develop. It helped to take a deep breath, stop a minute, and try to look at the situation from my husband's perspective, but that was also very difficult to do in the middle of it all. Being honest with each other and looking at my mistakes objectively helped me to take full responsibility when I needed to do so. Again, everyone has misunderstandings. When I made a mistake, I had to extend grace and forgive myself. Alternately, when my husband made a mistake, I had to extend grace to him also. This wasn't easy but became easier when I started looking clearly at myself. I knew I wasn't always doing things intentionally, so it wasn't fair to assume he was. I didn't want him always taking my mistakes personally, so it wasn't fair for me to do that either. I had to start taking responsibility for my actions as a way to learn and grow closer to my husband so I would not see his mistakes as personal character flaws. This helped us to move past challenges quicker and strengthened our relationship. We began to destroy resentment and build trust and accountability. In the end, it stopped the blame game.

YOUR TURN

We have all played the blame game at some point in our marriage. Think about the last time you blamed your spouse for something. How could you have handled that situation differently (even if your spouse was at fault in your opinion).

_____

_____

_____

What are practical ways you can intentional make your personal actions towards your spouse loving?

_____

_____

_____

What benefits do you anticipate in your marriage/relationship by taking more responsibility for your actions?

_____

_____

_____

I QUIT THINKING IT
WAS ALL ABOUT ME

"Then the LORD God said, 'It is not good for the man to be alone. I will make a helper who is just right for him.'"

—Genesis 2:18 (NLT)

Although I am of great value to my marriage and my family, I had to realize this wasn't about me, my marriage, or even my relationship with my children. It was so much bigger than me. There was a season in our marriage when I had gotten to a point of serious frustration with my husband. His quirkiness, his habit of forgetting, and his inability to read my mind were really upsetting me. I had gotten my inner voice back, and boy, was I vocal! I was saying and doing things contradictory to the reason he fell in love with me in the first place. He loved me at thirteen years old because I was interested in him. I didn't care about how he looked or what he did or didn't have. It didn't matter who his parents were or who he hung around. (We had only recently met, and I didn't know his family and friends from anyone else at that time.) I liked him for who he was! I was attracted to *him*! And now, "being him" wasn't enough. We had known each other for nearly thirty years. I needed to realize he wasn't fourteen anymore, and he wasn't and should not have been the same *him*.

However, I felt trapped in a marriage and relationship I was not happy with. At least, I thought I wasn't happy. I didn't realize it then, but that wasn't really about me either. It was all a plot, a plan made by the enemy to kill my husband. The enemy knew if he could bring my husband down, I would be heartbroken. But even bigger than my heartbreak, my husband's assignment would not be fulfilled on Earth, and neither would mine. I don't mean I was physically killing him. However, without realizing it, I was killing him mentally, emotionally, and spiritually with my words. No, I wasn't yelling and screaming and being disrespectful, but in my quest to voice my opinions and concerns, I wasn't speaking positively to him either. The tactic was to magnify and illuminate the things that frustrated, annoyed, and aggravated me as it related to my husband. I was blind to anything positive he said or did. What once attracted me to him now annoyed me to pieces. There was nothing apparently wrong—no one was cheating, and the sex was good. I simply couldn't stand being in the same room with him. If he forgot to take the trash out, I responded as though he had started a landfill in the middle of my living room.

I remember praying one day and asking God what was going on. That's when I realized this was bigger than me. My realization? My husband was sent to Earth with a mandate to bring change to young and old. He was sent to encourage, inspire, and impact diverse races and cultures. If our marriage could be a distraction from that, then Satan himself would feel as though he had gotten a victory over us. He would feel he could abort Jonathan's assignment. We were joined together as a couple at thirteen and fourteen years old not because of a crush and not because of teenage hormones, goo-goo eyes, or innocent butterflies. Not even because of the *Yes* box that was on the note he sent to me at youth camp. We were put together for a much bigger purpose. We were hand-picked by God to bring hope, healing, and restoration to marriages and relationships around the world. God destined us for *you* many years ago.

Then, God reminded me of the open vision I had at sixteen years old. I was sitting on my twin-sized bed in my girly girl bedroom at my mom's house—the one with the white furniture, the pink-and-white comforter and accessories, and plenty of stuffed animals and teddy bears (because that's what I was into then). As I lay on the bed with my head slightly hanging off the bottom, I saw Jonathan and myself on a stage. We were actually talking to a group of people about dating. There were hundreds of people in the room. In a quick scene switch, we were talking to thousands of married couples in a larger arena. To be honest, from the moment I'd had the vision as a teenager and spoken briefly to Jonathan about it over the phone, I had not even thought about it again until God reminded me of it those twenty-five years later. I wondered, why would God bring that memory to me *now*? I was over Jonathan. I had nothing to share with anyone about marriage or dating, or so I thought.

I had my voice, which was good and necessary, but knowing my value wasn't about me. Nor was my marriage, my relationship with my family, or my relationship and friendship with my husband about me. Our marriage was bigger than the two of us. I didn't get my voice back so I could control my husband, yell, or fuss, nor was it even to stand up for myself and make demands. I got my voice back so I could stand in agreement with my husband and stand up for marriages around the world. Together we could make a stance for *Kingdom Marriage*, the institution of husband and wife as God ordained in Genesis 2.

When I got a revelation of why God had us together according to Genesis 2, it changed my entire perspective of where I was in my marriage and what had been happening all those years.

> "Then the LORD God said, 'It is not good for the man to be alone. I will make a helper who is just right for him'" (Genesis 2:18 NLT).

One translation says, "...a helper as his complement." Instead of focusing on *complement* or even the word *comparable* (also used in other translations), let's look at the word *helper*. Here, *helper* is the Hebrew word *ezer* (ay-zer), which means to come to the aid of someone or to provide a service for someone—to supply what is missing or lacking. God did not give you another you, nor did He give Adam another Adam. He gave him someone who could supply what was lacking in Adam, and He gave you someone who could supply what is lacking in you. Your spouse is not going to mirror you because Earth already has you. You need someone who is going to complement you.

For example, ketchup and mustard complement each other. They are great separately and have distinctive tastes. Ketchup has a sweetness to it while mustard has a very bold hint of vinegar and punch. Together, they create something neither of them can produce separately. Eve was created to complement Adam. In the same way, your spouse (if you allowed God to put you together) was created to complement you.

So, I am his complement. If I am "just right for him," then why did I feel like we were totally incompatible? The reality, whether I wanted to admit it or not, was that we were incomplete, unhealed young people looking for a spouse or companion who would come along and fix "it." Instead, I ended up on a journey with the very one who would drive me insane (if I rebelled against the plan and agenda of God). The problem was that I didn't even know what it meant to be compatible. I only looked at compatibility as how similar two things or people are when in definition it means to be capable of existing or living together in harmony. It is to be able to exist together with something or someone else, to be consistent.

Being compatible didn't mean I had to be exactly like my husband, but what made us compatible was that we had the same beliefs, values, and character. We can be compatible but totally different. God hand-picked Jonathan for me and me for Jonathan. God knew I needed Jonathan in my life so I could be healed. He knew I needed Jonathan to cause me to take the journey back to and through my past so I could properly heal from the wounds of my past with His guidance. God also knew that because we were so different as individual people, I would never choose to be with Jonathan, and he would never choose to be with me. So, He wired our brains to release certain chemicals and hormones to trick us into falling in love and see past all the flaws each of us had. When I met him, because of the little hormone cocktail party going on in my brain, I thought I was with Jonathan because he was going to take me away from and fix all of my childhood hurts.

I never knew he would cause me to look at all my flaws, dig up all my past hurts, and uncover all my past wounds so they could be healed. No, not Jonathan. He was going to rescue me, and we were going to live happily ever after. After all, we had all of the proof of young love. My heart would flutter whenever we were together. I would spend endless hours on the phone talking to him (I would literally talk to him until the sun came up some mornings), sharing our dreams of our future together. Whenever I drove to see him, I would get butterflies the closer I got to his house. That was the proof we needed to show we were really in love, right?

Well, that was short-lived. As many marriages do, our marriage started with loving, honoring, and protecting one another and moved to misunderstanding and hurting each other. We were deeply damaging each other through our words and actions. We would often consider and vocalize divorce. At one point, my husband actually put me out of our home. (See his chapter: "I Quit Controlling My Marriage.") We soon committed to removing this option, however, and took the word *divorce* off the table and out of our vocabulary. Yet, we still ended up living together as damaged, hurt, and broken individuals. We had wounds from our past, we had wounds from each other, and we had fresh wounds from our present. We often touched each other's wounds, and this caused disagreements, arguments, and fights.

You know the old saying "opposites attract"? Well, studies have proven it to be true. Dr. Susan Campbell studied hundreds of couples and found we fall in love with the most incompatible people in the world. In fact, we fall in love with the people most capable of causing us pain and least capable of meeting our primary human needs. However, that's the very person who God knew would stretch you and cause you to grow. This is not comparable to physical pain, violence, or abuse. I am not advocating staying in a relationship that physically harms you. I am, rather, referring to the pain that comes with growth. They will be the very one to push your buttons enough to cause you to grow and expand to the person you were destined to be. Now, tell the truth: if you knew this about your future spouse, would you have even given them the time of day? If you knew they would cause you to face the very things you were uncomfortable with, things you never wanted to look at or mention again, the very things that caused you hurt and pain, you would run the other way. I know I would have. Be honest. Would you have agreed to face it? Well, if you are anything like me, you would not have bothered with it but would have gone the other way too.

We spent many years wondering what was going on and trying to fix the wrong thing because we were blaming the wrong thing. It was many years into our marriage before we learned the truth.

So, how did I feel he was my prince charming for so long? My brain literally drugged me. In fact, it's how God made us. When I learned the scientific truth behind how God strategically wired us, it made sense, and things began to change. Since that point in our marriage, we have built connection, stability, security, and genuine love for each other. So, how did we end up together? Our brains release chemicals like phenylethylamine, oxytocin, and dopamine, allowing us to fall in love and see each other through a filter. God wired us to choose our spouse based on His will for our lives. When you fall in love, you see your similarities and tend to ignore your differences. You see the things that were compatible, alike, and positive in the relationship. Although the negative and incompatible traits may have arisen, you ignored these. You did what you needed to do to please your partner and have them like you. Even the differences that stick out do not appear to be a big deal when these chemical levels are high.

When all of that calmed down (the levels balanced out), it was as though a fog had lifted. I woke up one day well into my marriage and suddenly realized how different we were from each other. As a matter of fact, I felt how all of the sacrifices I had made in our dating relationship and even in our marriage had hindered me from doing what I wanted to do in life. Before I realized it, the things that once caused me to fall so in love with my husband, the things I once bragged about, and even the things I once could overlook as *not so bad* annoyed me to no end. I had no problem letting him know exactly how annoyed and bothered I was. I didn't feel like he was my safe place anymore.

Instead of viewing him as the solution to my problems, I saw him as the central cause of them. We began to disconnect in our relationship, and I felt unappreciated and uncertain. I would become extremely needy on some days, and on other days I was shut down and withdrawn from him. The bliss was officially gone, but I didn't know what had happened. It was as though we had fallen out of love with each other, or at least I had fallen out of love with him. I wanted more in my life. I had pushed him, his dream, and his purpose for so long that I had forgotten about mine. My desires had sat on the back burner far too long. I was so unaware of what was happening under the surface of my marriage, my relationship, and the core of my character. I didn't understand how God was using situations and circumstances with my husband and me to heal me from what I thought was so far behind me. Jonathan and I were literally touching each other's wounds from the past, and it was causing us to fight against each other because we simply didn't know. We had no understanding of what we were doing. Every time Jonathan got close to my wounds, I would reject him and act out of character, and he was doing the same. When we both realized how wounded and hurt we were, we sought help. We were able to seek professional help in processing through old baggage, and this helped us to see what was really happening beneath the surface. We became each other's safe places again. He was able to express himself with me, and I was able to express myself to him without either of us taking it personally or feeling attacked. That was life-changing and liberating. It was healing.

I realized not only am I in this marriage to help other marriages one day, but I am in this marriage to help bring healing to my husband so he can complete his assignment on Earth. How exactly did I bring healing to him? Honor. Honor heals men. How did he heal me? He started putting me first. He returned to cherishing me at a time when I felt unappreciated and devalued, which made me feel loved and appreciated again.

I had to begin to celebrate my husband as the person God intended for me: my exact opposite. I began to allow him to heal me in the most vulnerable places. That's how God wired me. Although I had no clue of this when that chemical cocktail was in full effect while we were dating and in the earlier years of our marriage, it was clear now. We vowed again to not only love each other and heal each other throughout the remainder of our years of marriage together, but we vowed also to cherish one another. We vowed to value our differences and the ways we complement each other. We fell out of love only to fall back in love. This time it was with clarity and stability coupled with a mature romance, mature intimacy, mutual respect, and honor for each other. This time it was real, cherished love.

YOUR TURN

What is your spouse's God given purpose?

_____

_____

_____

How can/or how do you compliment your spouse in their purpose?

_____

_____

_____

I QUIT LOVING HIM BY DEFINITION ONLY

"Be devoted to one another in love. Honor one another above yourselves."

—Romans 12:10 NIV

I love you! Love you! Love ya! Love you more! We've all heard and said this phrase in its many different variations and on different occasions to a variety of people with different bonds and various personal connections. We love our spouse, our children, and our parents and siblings. We love our coworkers and those with whom we worship as well as our neighbors. We love our pets, our cousins, extended family members, and our friends. As you see, this list could easily continue. We love a lot of different people, places, and things in many different ways, or at least we *say* we do.

I found myself questioning my love for my husband. We had been married for years, and we were successful in our careers and businesses, but I had begun to wonder and ask myself, "Do I really love him?" When I asked myself the question, it was hard to answer with a *yes*. So, I grabbed a dictionary and began to look at the definition of the word *love*. What is love, really? According to Webster's dictionary, love is an intense feeling, a deep affection for something or someone. It is a great interest and pleasure in something. In action form, love is the act of feeling a deep romantic or sexual attachment to someone. I looked further and saw more definitions that included love as a variety of feelings, emotions, and attitudes. It is an emotional attachment.

With these definitions alone my claim was indeed substantiated. I didn't truly love him anymore. I was no longer interested in him. I didn't have deep feelings of affection. I didn't even have any deep romantic or sexual attachment. So, I started filling my own head with false thoughts and statements as many people do. Those thoughts included, "He deserves someone better than me," and "He deserves someone who can love him for who he is." That obviously was not me, right? I had one more source to consider. *The* source. When I looked at God's definition of love, I was immediately convicted. I had been trying to love my husband in all the wrong ways. I Corinthians 13:4-8 (NIV) describes the real definition of love:

> Love is patient, love is kind. It does not envy, it does not boast, it is not proud. It does not dishonor others, it is not self-seeking, it is not easily angered, it keeps no record of wrongs. Love does not delight in evil but rejoices with the truth. It

always protects, always trusts, always hopes, always perseveres. Love never fails.

If God is love and we are to be like Him, then I needed to try His definition of love. After all, I made the vow to love until death do us part.

So, I took a different perspective on loving Jonathan. I put myself into the scripture. Ayanna is patient, Ayanna is kind. She does not envy, she does not boast, she is not proud. She does not dishonor others, she is not self-seeking, she is not easily angered, she keeps no record of wrongs. She does not delight in evil but rejoices with the truth. She always protects, always trusts, always hopes, always perseveres. Ayanna never fails.

Whoa. In a perfect world, I could say that was a complete and honest depiction of me. At least it was what some people observed on the outside, but it was not really me, not consistently. I could not wholeheartedly agree that Ayanna was love. I portrayed some of the characteristics of love in some areas but certainly not all according to the biblical view. More often than not I was the exact opposite of love. It is not easy to stop and do a complete and honest self-evaluation, but I had to look in the mirror and make a decision. Could I do this? Would I try? I decided I wholeheartedly desired to love my husband the way God intended me to love, the way God commissioned me to love him, the way God laid it out for me to love. But realistically how could I? As painful as the truth was, I was far from this ideal.

That's when God showed me what was missing. As I laid across the bottom of my bed that fall evening, asking God to answer the hard question, I knew my husband was a good man. I knew my husband had a good heart. I knew my husband was integral to my life and an all-around great guy. He loved God and had a pure heart toward the things of God. He was literally the epitome of a "man after God's own heart." I didn't know why it had gotten so hard to love him. As much as I wanted to and as much as I prayed for a new grace to take our love to a new level, the hard answer was, *Yanna, you can't!* You can't love your husband the way you think you desire to because you no longer cherish him. You are seeking to love him, but you should be working on cherishing him. That was it. I didn't vow to love til death do us part. I vowed to love *and cherish* til death do us part. I had forgotten about that part. I had placed all of my emphasis on loving him and totally overlooked how I was so very far from cherishing him. I could not love him without cherishing him. If I wanted our love to be repaired so we could go to the next level, I had to cherish him *again.* To cherish is to appreciate, to hold something dear, to treasure it, to protect it, to honor, and to adore something or someone. God told me how learning to cherish him again would not only strengthen our marriage, it would transform our marriage and our relationship as a whole. It would deepen what we had for each other, and we would see each other in a new light.

I had cherished him once before, but I wasn't doing so at this particular time. After years of dating and marriage, after years of being parents and business owners, paying bills, making budgets, and handling the daily operations of life, home, family, church, school, jobs, etc., we had moved from loving and cherishing to taking each other for granted. We were living on auto-pilot. I no longer protected my husband's character. I no longer protected his heart but fell into the societal way of downplaying what I had with my husband. I stopped honoring. I ceased showing gratitude to and for him. I stopped noticing what was important. I no longer respected what we had and stopped holding him dear. He simply became another everyday thing. I allowed the value of our relationship, the value of what our unique union produced, to be devalued; I stopped cherishing him.

What does cherishing look like biblically? We look at 1 Corinthians 13 to see what love looks and feels like. If we look at Song of Songs 1 (ESV), Solomon and his bride show us what it looks and feels like to be cherished by our spouse.

The Song of Songs, which is Solomon's:

She
> Let him kiss me with the kisses of his mouth!
> For your love is better than wine;
> your anointing oils are fragrant;
> your name is oil poured out;
> therefore virgins love you.
> Draw me after you; let us run.
> The king has brought me into his chambers.

Others
> We will exult and rejoice in you;
> we will extol your love more than wine;
> rightly do they love you.

She
> I am very dark, but lovely, O daughters of Jerusalem,
> like the tents of Kedar,
> like the curtains of Solomon. Do not gaze at me because I am dark, because the sun has looked upon me. My mother's sons were angry with me; they made me keeper of the vineyards, but my own vineyard I have not kept! Tell me, you whom my soul loves, where you pasture your flock, where you make it lie down at noon;

for why should I be like one who veils herself beside the flocks of your companions?

He

If you do not know, O most beautiful among women, follow in the tracks of the flock, and pasture your young goats beside the shepherds' tents.

I compare you, my love, to a mare among Pharaoh's chariots. Your cheeks are lovely with ornaments, your neck with strings of jewels.

Others

We will make for you ornaments of gold, studded with silver.

She

While the king was on his couch, my nard gave forth its fragrance.
My beloved is to me a sachet of myrrh that lies between my breasts. My beloved is to me a cluster of henna blossoms in the vineyards of Engedi.

He

Behold, you are beautiful, my love; behold, you are beautiful; your eyes are doves.

She

Behold, you are beautiful, my beloved, truly delightful. Our couch is green;
the beams of our house are cedar; our rafters are pine.

God intended for husbands and wives to cherish each other. It's not simply a vow that has been passed down for generations. As far back as medieval times, married couples have stood before God and a host of family, friends, and guests and made promises to each other. These vows were first documented and printed in the first book of common prayer.

Even further, God cherishes us. David describes how it feels to be loved and cherished by God in Psalms 139:1-18:

> O LORD, you have searched me and known me!
> You know when I sit down and when I rise up;
> you discern my thoughts from afar.
> You search out my path and my lying down and
> are acquainted with all my ways. Even before a
> word is on my tongue, behold, O LORD, you know
> it altogether. You hem me in, behind and before,
> and lay your hand upon me.
> Such knowledge is too wonderful for me; it is high;
> I cannot attain it.
> Where shall I go from your Spirit? Or where shall
> I flee from your presence?
> If I ascend to heaven, you are there! If I make my
> bed in Sheol, you are there!
> If I take the wings of the morning and dwell in
> the uttermost parts of the sea,
> even there your hand shall lead me, and your right
> hand shall hold me.
> If I say, "Surely the darkness shall cover me, and
> the light about me be night,"
> even the darkness is not dark to you; the night is
> bright as the day,
> for darkness is as light with you. For you formed
> my inward parts;
> you knitted me together in my mother's womb.
> I praise you, for I am fearfully and wonderfully
> made. Wonderful are your works; my soul knows
> it very well. My frame was not hidden from you,
> when I was being made in secret,
> intricately woven in the depths of the earth. Your
> eyes saw my unformed substance; in our book

were written, every one of them, the days that were formed for me, when as yet there was none of them. How precious to me are your thoughts, O God! How vast is the sum of them!
If I would count them, they are more than the sand. I awake, and I am still with you.

For every instruction God gives, He not only gives examples. He Himself exemplifies it to us. When my eyes opened to what needed to happen, my marriage transformed, and our relationship went to an entirely different level. We now share a love, relationship, and marriage that is the most authentic and genuine it has ever been. We can be honest with each other without resentment or hurt. We are able to be real. We can be our true selves without fear of judgment or rejection. There is mutual honor, respect, and admiration for each other. I don't mind showcasing my marriage and my husband to others, and doing so makes him feel even more cherished. We have created a culture of cherishing that spirals down to our children and throughout our home. We are loving to cherish! We've made the *Vow2Cherish™*!

YOUR TURN

In what ways do you love your spouse?

_____

In what ways do you cherish your spouse?

_____

In what ways do you feel loved by your spouse?

_____

In what ways do you feel cherished by your spouse?

_____

In what ways do you feel loved by God?

_____

In what ways do you feel cherished by God?

_____

CPSIA information can be obtained
at www.ICGtesting.com
Printed in the USA
FSHW010411230121
77931FS

Redefining your perspective can take you from *I quit* to *I refuse to quit.*

Though marriage can be one of the best decisions you make in life, it often starts far from the happily ever after seen in fairytales. However, there is great love and fulfillment with marriage between a couple committed to doing the work.

- What happens when the bliss wears off?
- What happens when proclivities and old habits keep your marriage at a standstill?
- How do you handle feeling that your marriage is in a cycle of defeat or regret?
- Did you ever think you'd wonder, Who am I married to, and why?

When challenges with burn out, exhaustion, and defeat replace love and romance, many throw in the towel and declare, *"I QUIT!"*

The marriage journey was just as difficult for Jonathan & Ayanna. They share their roadmap for overcoming hurt, rejection, self-sabotage, and destruction while offering tested and proven strategies that will guide your marriage. No matter the stage, all (considering marriage, engaged, newlywed, veteran couples, troubled marriages, or even good relationships) can benefit from these essential tools.

With passion and insight from the science of psychology and their faith, you will experience dual perspectives as you travel with the Kilgores. They can help you

recognize areas in your life and marriage that need to be abandoned. These strategies will challenge you and create the agents of change.

Rekindle the fire, restore the love,
and reinvent your marriage,
when walking away seems the best option.
Allow your marriage to be saved!

GENTLEMEN NEXT
JONATHAN'S PERSPECTIVE

1994

1997

I QUIT COMPLAINING

"When doubt comes against us, we have to lift up the shield of faith. We do this when we open our mouth and say what God's word says, rather than grumbling and complaining about the problem."

—Joyce Meyer

Our words have the ability to create, develop, tear down, and destroy. Solomon showed us proof of this in Proverbs 18:21(NLT) when he said, "The tongue can bring death or life; those who love to talk will reap the consequences." I had to stop allowing myself to use my tongue and my words to complain about my situation and my wife. Instead, I started using my words to accentuate the positive, the good in what I had and in what was going on.

Even though I have heard it most of my life and have said most of my life that I should look like God and want to be like God, I wasn't truly like God in the

way I spoke. God gave us the ultimate example of using words to create. Look at the first chapter of Genesis: "In the beginning God created the heaven and the earth . . . and God said, Let there be light: and there was light" (Genesis 1;1, 1:3 KJV). No, I am *not* God, but I am created in His image and His likeness, and I strive to be more and more like Him every day. If He used His words to create, I can use mine to create as well.

It takes lots of practice to be able to speak the right thing. It takes practice to program ourselves to choose to say the positive things and not the negative even when the situation presented is negative. I used to complain about my wife a lot. I would complain to my pastor, and I would complain to my coworkers. (I worked at the church we both attended.) I would complain to my friends. "She doesn't talk unless she wants to talk; it's like she always has walls up. She's not loving me the way I want to be loved. She only makes love when she wants to make love. She's not submissive. She's not a team player. She just gets on my nerves." They would tell me I needed to give her consequences for what she was doing. I needed to *make* her do what I wanted her to do. I needed to ride out on her with another woman so she would see the effects of what she was doing. Those suggestions were not going to make our marriage better. They may have succeeded in making me feel better temporarily, but in the end it would have been much more destructive than helpful.

I would say things like "I don't like you, but I love you." Wow! I had no idea what I was doing by saying that, but I was creating walls between us and tearing down the walls that were behind us. I spent most of my life speaking things as I saw them instead of speaking in faith based on what God had shown and promised me about her. It was when I changed what I was saying

that I started to see things change. It has taken me years to get this down to the point where it comes out naturally. I have learned to put pressure on my mouth and to challenge and train my tongue to speak the promises of God. I want to challenge you to use your words to create what you want to see. Your positive words can create the financial portfolio you want to have, and your negative words can create the opposite effect. If you want the intimacy, romance, and sex to increase and get better, start speaking that. Don't talk about what he is not doing or what she is not doing. Instead, talk about what you desire from your spouse. "She's a great lover." "He meets all my needs." "She knows how to touch me in all the right places." "He knows the right words to say to me at the right times to turn me on." Even if your wife is coming to bed in flannel pajamas or your husband is wearing run down gym shorts, share with her what you like and tell him what you desire. Speak it into the atmosphere. Speak it to your spouse. Maybe have some nice lingerie laying out for your wife or something sexy for your husband to put on. Add a spicy note to it. Speak it and let your actions cosign with what you are speaking and desiring.

If we share our desires with our spouses as much or more than we share our complaints and dissatisfactions, we will start to see a difference. It may not happen overnight, but don't get tired of speaking positively. It is easy to complain and take the negative role, but it is challenging to say the right thing, the positive thing. Speak life over your spouse as God's word encourages us to do by speaking positive confessions and affirmations to and about them.

I remember sitting in a teacher training years ago. My wife and I owned several daycares, and we would have staff development teacher trainings. In this particular

training, my wife was teaching about classroom management. I remember she told the teachers that when you make rules for your classroom, tell the children what you *want* them to do instead of what you *do not* want them to do. When you tell them what you want them to do, that's what they will remember. A child's brain typically holds onto the last action word they hear. So, if you tell a child, "Walk in the building," they will hear *walk*. If you tell a child, "Don't run in the building," they are going to hear *run*! And that's likely the response you will get every time.

If your spouse hears you talking about what you don't want, what they're doing wrong, or what is bothering you all the time, that is likely what is going to take residence in their mind. Those words will start to surface or remain in your relationship. Alternatively, if you speak what you desire, then that is what you will experience.

I remember a time earlier in our marriage when Ayanna and I lived in a townhouse with our two children at the time. We were at a point in our marriage where it seemed like nothing we did was working and we were not going to make it. We had a disagreement about something, and it got to the point where I told her to get out. Her name was not on the lease, and I told her to get out of *my* house if she couldn't "act right." She refused to leave (for obvious reasons), so I called the police to make her leave. I was so angry with her and was trying to make a point to her. I told the police, "Hey, if she's not going to act right, she's got to go." *Act right*, as though she were a child. We were young in our marriage and very immature. It didn't look like there was any hope for us. This had to have been one of the closest times to divorce we had ever come.

We were constantly at each other and could never agree. So, Ayanna left the house at the advice of the

officer. She was hurt and in disbelief that I actually called the police and was going through with making her vacate the premises. I thought I had succeeded in making my point, but I succeeded in a lot more than that. I had built a wall between us. Once, there was a wall around us with a window between us to create boundaries and to protect our deepest emotions and connections from the outside. Now, that wall was coming between us. With every complaint I made to someone about my wife, I opened a window to that person, and with every complaint and put-down I made about my wife, especially with this trick I'd pulled, I was building a wall between us.

Ayanna took the children (though I didn't know at the time) and went to a friend's house to stay. She had the clothes on her back and the purse in her hand—that's it. She changed the children's daycare, and I had no idea where they were. Even though I called, at this point she was not coming back. One day, my mother-in-law called me, and I remember her asking me what was going on. I shared with her what was happening, and she said, "Well, Jonathan, somebody has to be the bigger person. Somebody has to do the right thing." It was her words that caused me to go into prayer, repent for what I had done, and call my wife to ask her forgiveness as well. I went downstairs, and I remember listening to a gospel artist who had a song out called "Rhema Word." The lyrics of that song got my attention. I listened to it over and over as I prayed. I told God I needed to hear from Him. I remember God telling me clear as day we were going to make it. My wife and I were not going to separate, nor would we get a divorce. Things were going to turn, and they would be great.

I eventually convinced Ayanna to come home and talk to me. She came home, but her attitude toward me

had not changed. Her decision had not changed. She had no interest in what I was going to say. I grabbed her, looked her in the eye, and told her, "I am not going anywhere, and you are not either," but she was adamant that she was leaving. She was preparing to permanently move out and file for legal separation. In her words, she was done. For those who know my wife, you know it is very dangerous to hear Ayanna say she is done. She will tolerate a lot, but when she is *done* with something, it takes God and all the hosts of angels to cause her to give it attention again. It could be situations, conversations, relationships, people, friends, or foes. When she's done, *she's done*, and she was done with our marriage. She was especially done with me, but I had the assurance of what God had promised me. I could not shake it. I could not let the words God had given me go.

Ayanna came back home but stayed in the kid's room. She needed time to save her money until her next payday, and then she was moving out. The next week, I got the miracle I had been waiting for. Ayanna went to the doctor and found out she was eight weeks pregnant. She had been pregnant all this time, and we hadn't known. She was angry, upset, and confused. But my wife is very smart, and she told me, "We are going to have to figure this out. I ain't raising three kids on my own while you go free." My youngest daughter was and is a miracle baby to me. No, there was never anything wrong with her physically or as it related to the pregnancy or her health. But because of the conception of this beautiful baby, my marriage had hope. My wife and I named her Jadyn, which means "God has heard." And God *did* hear. He heard my prayers and granted my desires.

That was the hinge on which our marriage swung and changed. Not the birth exactly, but the conception

of a baby changed the trajectory of my marriage. I thank God for swinging it and changing it. I spoke His word, and He changed our track. I was in a hopeless situation, but I put pressure on my mouth and spoke what God said to speak.

Prior to that, I was speaking what I saw, and I began to see more of it because that was what my words were creating. As hard as it was to admit, everything I saw in my wife was because my words were creating and recreating it every time I complained. I put those words in the atmosphere even when I was simply describing what was going on. My words and thoughts were negative, and they manifested as a negative environment. When I complained, my words had me in a place of extreme fear and extreme anxiety. I was on the verge of losing my wife and my family over a situation I had created with my words. That was a tough pill to swallow, but it was the truth. When we speak, we begin to believe it and to see it. That includes complaints.

My words changed and with them my thoughts, and once I had modified my thoughts, I was able to change in other positive ways. During this transition, my life began to improve, and with each positive life choice I made, my wife also began to grow. As Ayanna began to change, our children also improved, and before I knew it, my entire household was transforming.

God has promised us an abundance, and we have assurance because of His promise. We simply need to make sure everything that comes out of our mouths aligns with what God said and what He says in His word. Not only should we speak positively and speak our desires, but we should also write out Gods promises and plan for our lives. "Write the vision, and make it plain upon tables, that he may run that readeth it" (Habakkuk 2:2). I like the way this verse reads in the

Good News Translation: "Write down clearly on tablets what I reveal to you, so that it can be read at a glance."

Individual promises, the promises you have as a couple, and household promises should all be included. Write down the promises and desires you have for your personal life, professional life, even ministry. Write them clearly and concisely so you can read them at a glance and keep them at the forefront of your mind. Post them in a place, or several places, so that you can glance at them daily; multiple times a day. And even if it takes a long time, believe in it and trust that it is going to happen. How do I know? Because God told Habakkuk, "Put it in writing, because it is not yet time for it to come true. But the time is coming quickly, and what I show you will come true. It may seem slow in coming, but wait for it; it will certainly take place, and it will not be delayed (Habakkuk 2:2 GNT).

YOUR TURN

Write three goals for each category below. Create the life you desire.

Husband (Individual)

_____

_____

_____

Wife (Individual)

_____

_____

_____

Couple Goals

_____

_____

_____

Household Goals

_____

_____

_____

I QUIT CONTROLLING MY MARRIAGE

*"But now, O LORD, you are our Father; we are the clay,
and you are our potter;
we are all the work of your hand."*

—Isaiah 64:8 (ESV)

For a large part of my marriage, I tried to control all the outcomes of most situations we faced. I tried to control how things *would* go based on the way I thought things *should* go. With my false assumptions and thoughts that the man was the "head of the house," I thought I had to control everything and make all of the decisions—from making love to going out and everything in between, I ruled over it. The best way to get the outcome I wanted was for me to micromanage it (or so I thought). I realized after many years

of unproductiveness and not seeing the results I was expecting that this way was not accomplishing much; my eyes were opened. I was leading the house instead of letting the Holy Spirit control and lead the house. Growing up, I heard sermon after sermon and teaching after teaching stating the man was the head of the house. Men were in charge. Men were in control and called the shots in their home, and any man who didn't was ridiculed and publicly shamed. The truth of the matter is, even though God structured man as the head of the house and head of the family, God is the head of the unit. In order for my wife and I to see a perfect flow, I had to not only understand how God flowed and allow Him to lead. I had to understand who I was and who God created me to be. I had to figure out and break down the operating components of my control.

FEAR

I was afraid of how things would play out and where our relationship would go if I didn't keep control of it.

TRUST

I didn't trust how things might turn out if I gave up control. I didn't have the necessary faith in God to have it under control to do things the way He wanted. I didn't even trust Ayanna because of past hurts, situations, and disappointments. I simply didn't want to be hurt anymore. I didn't want to be disappointed anymore.

FAILURE

Past failures were significant in stopping me from releasing control. I never wanted to experience what I had felt in my prior experiences with failure.

I was unaware of how much I was being robbed. My need to control my situation was stopping me from being able to enjoy the flow of my marriage, but I didn't recognize what was happening. It was hindering me from finding and experiencing the full joy of marriage and my relationship with my wife in general.

When I looked at the relationship of the Trinity, it helped me see how my relationship with my wife was supposed to flow and operate. The relationship between God the Father, God the Son, and God the Spirit is such that though they are one, they are triune. There is so much passion, love, trust, and confidence in each other. The roles are defined and known. The paths and plans are distinct for each role. Without thinking about it, they flow in their distinct roles—Father, Son, and the Holy Spirit—effortlessly. They are able to trust and depend on each other. They support each other in their efforts to love God's people. In creation, after Jesus ascended, the Holy Spirit came as another form of Him.

If we are made in the image and likeness of God, our marriages should be a reflection of God's relationship with the church. Our marriages and relationships should be able to flow like that of the Trinity. We should be able to move with such preciseness, knowing our roles, knowing when one moves in and the other moves out. We should be able to trust each other and flow with each other effortlessly. There should be great passion in our relationships.

I am a musician, and I have traveled extensively—locally, nationally, and internationally—working with a

lot of different groups. I have had experience in groups where I attempted to lead and be in control, trying to make it go the way the leader wanted it to go without regard to musicianship or skill. We may have even had several practice sessions before the "gig" to make sure everything was right. I have also been in bands, organized bands, and seen bands where the musicians flow without even thinking. These are honestly the best groups. Sometimes their first time playing together wasn't until the day or night of the performance. There was such chemistry that the musicians were able to simply flow. When this happens, there is great energy created on the stage. You can hear the chord progression before it gets there; you can anticipate it and flow with it. No instruction is needed. The keyboardist, vocalist, bass player, sax player, and anyone else in the band simply knows where to go. Nothing has been rehearsed, and no cues are given. We feel each other on the stage. You can feel the beat of the drummer, the pulse of the bass guitar, and the melody of the acoustic guitar. There is a consistent flow. Everybody is leaning on each other, trusting each other, and trusting the groove. Everyone on the stage knows their role. For a musician or band, this is the perfect moment. There is nothing else like it.

We had to get our marriage into the perfect groove, a groove where we were able to flow without cues or instructions. But in order for us to find our groove, I had to release control. I had to learn to give God full control in my marriage. I had to give up what I wanted and pray God would actually start bringing us into harmony with one beat and one voice. It took time, effort, patience, trust, and passion to get us here. In order for us to have complete harmony, we both had to give up control. This included our finances, our children—everything. We are on the same heartbeat, and we have the same pulse.

We are together. We are walking and moving forward together; our vision is aligned.

We both had to be open to trusting each other because giving up control requires trust and vulnerability, trust being the firm belief in the reliability, truth, ability, and strength of my wife. It was being able to allow someone to have, use, or look after something I valued with complete confidence. I had to be able to believe that if I fell, my wife would be there to catch me (or at least make her best effort to try) no matter what! I now believe my wife would be there with her arms out and would make every effort to help me if I stumbled, to steady me if I tripped, and to catch me if I fell. I can depend on that. I have faith in that. Even if I'm not in the room, even when I'm not around, I know my wife supports me and has my back. I also know she will come through and communicate with me what she needs as well so I can do the same for her. I trust that if I hurt my wife, she will forgive me as I can forgive her, and we will move on from that place. It took getting to that level of trust to be able to release control.

Even in the band, we needed trust. It takes trust for the leader to be able to give the keyboardist, the guitarist, or the drummer time for their solo. I trust the drummer can take on the rhythm or a beat and lead the entire band into another groove without me controlling him or telling him where to go. We simply trust his lead.

I can trust my wife to know when it's time for her to lead, and she knows when it's time for me to guide. If my wife is skilled in something or has grace in an area, I allow her to hear God and shepherd us in that moment. Vice versa, when I have skills and grace in a particular area, that's when I step up. I trust her enough to have confidence in her *know* and her *no*. She can also trust me enough to rely on my *know* and my *no*.

We both understand that the *no* is without ill motive or selfish intention. We both trust the *know* is being led by the Holy Spirit.

A lack of trust often leads to fear. In the Trinity, there is trust amongst the three. There is no room for fear within the trinity, and when we have trust in our marriage, there is no room for apprehension there either. When fear enters, it paralyzes. Many people are afraid to try new things or to follow someone else. They may be afraid to try a new restaurant or go to a different vacation destination, or they may be afraid to do things differently in their relationships. After being married for many years, you don't want to do the same things you did when you first got married—at least, you shouldn't want to. But fear can stop you from leaving your comfort zone. We ought to try different foods and do new things, and we can embrace new ways!

Your relationship should flow like a beautiful waterfall. No interruptions, only constant flow like a forceful cascade off the cliff—the ultimate flow.

There was a time in our marriage when I would try to control our conversations about issues or problems in the house. I'm the type of person who likes to talk about something as soon as it happens. I believe if we go ahead and talk about it, we can get everything out on the table, deal with it, and get over it. Ayanna, on the other hand, is the total opposite. She would rather process it, think about it, and then talk about it. Sometimes she would decide she didn't want to talk about it at all. In my fear of her not talking about it at all or going extended lengths of time before she could or would talk about it, I would try to control the situation and force her to talk. So, if she went into the room and closed the door, I would make my way into wherever she was and try to make her talk. If she locked the door, I would pick the

lock, enter, and try to make her talk, saying something like, "Hey, we need to talk. We need to talk now." If she tried to leave the house, I would stand in front of her or try to block her exits so she couldn't leave. I was afraid that if we didn't talk right then, we would never talk about it, and we would never solve the issue. I was also concerned that if she left, she would never come back. (See "We Quit Using the 'D' Word" for more on that.) I was fearful she wouldn't meet my needs. I was afraid she wouldn't be there if I needed to be hugged, needed to be loved, or wanted to make love because when she was mad or angry, none of that would happen.

I didn't realize then that shutting down was a safety mechanism for her. Her silent treatments were her way of saying, "What I can't see or hear won't hurt me." So, when I felt I needed to control how we would handle and discuss things, it made her angry, causing bitter fights. As a consequence, the situation would escalate further out of control, making the situation seem more severe than it actually was. My need for control caused more damage than good every time. I was damaging our relationship, and I was pushing her away from me, causing her to have a lack of trust in me. She was pushing me away in an attempt to control the situation in her own way.

I had to learn to understand my wife's communication style. She is not going to talk about most things on the spot. She needs time to process what was said and done. Not everyone is ready to process things right away. Some people need time, and she is one of those people. Instead of trying to force her to talk, I had to understand how she communicates. I got much better results when I gave her time—time to breathe, time to process, and time to deal with her emotions at that moment.

For myself, while she was going through her processing strategy, I had to learn to take care of myself and control what I could control: myself. I had to learn what self-awareness and self-care is. There were things I needed to do to help myself. We all have needs. If Ayanna wasn't meeting my needs, I had to take care of them. If that meant going to a nice restaurant by myself (as long as the food was good), I would do it. I would go to a place I love and get some of my favorite things to eat. If that meant going to the movie theater and watching a few movies, I would go from one movie to another and simply relax. Sometimes it meant going to the spa and getting a massage. Those were things I had to figure out about myself. It gave me practical things to do that I needed to sustain myself while I waited for Ayanna to get herself together and get in a place where she could talk.

Self-care really helped me to release the need to control. I realized some things were simply not mine to decide and had nothing to do with me. I had to release the issues and my wife to God—totally. Once I had done what I could do—apologize, share my heart, and tell her how I felt if she was still upset, angry, or in a mood—I had to accept there was nothing I could do about it. I had to come face to face with my own issues: fear, anger, and control. I had to leave the rest to God, and after doing that for quite some time, I noticed Ayanna was starting to change. But I wasn't changing her— the Holy Spirit was.

We learned how to communicate properly. We learned how to share when there were issues. We figured out how to talk so we understood each other. Earlier in our marriage, I would try to control the conversation, and when Ayanna was talking, I would try to control her. She would try to speak with me, but before she could

get her words out, I would try to finish her statement as though I already knew what her next words would be—only to be wrong ninety percent of the time. I never heard her because I had an outcome already in my mind. I heard what I wanted to hear or what I thought she would say. That caused her to shut down, and rightfully so. She didn't want to talk anymore because I wasn't allowing her to really speak. I expressed how I wanted to communicate, saying I wanted her to talk, but then I was controlling the conversation. In her words, I only wanted to hear myself talk because *I* wasn't listening to her anyway. I didn't realize I was doing that until she brought it to my attention. Then, when I did some self-reflection, I discovered I was doing that and worse. It had been done to me all my life growing up. As a child I was told,

"Shut up."

"You don't have anything to say about that."

"You can't say anything about that. Be quiet."

"Don't talk. I'm telling you what you are going to do, and I'm telling you how you feel."

Those experiences shaped me to respond the same way, not only with my wife but with other people in other relationships as well. This happened especially during heated moments. Without listening and without hearing her, I was preventing myself from getting to know her because I was controlling the conversation. I learned to be quiet and listen, and to come into a conversation without preconceived notions of what we were going to talk about. I had to start putting my feelings and my thoughts to the side to hear what she had to say. I learned I have a very educated wife with great ideas. After she finished talking, I would then respond to what she said not in defense but to make sure I clearly understood what she said. Then, I would

share what I had to say concerning the situation, and she would listen to what I had to say. Both of us would then come together with facts and information to find a resolution that worked for us. That's how we found our flow. That's how we found our groove.

I encourage you to take the brakes off of your relationship. Flow in your relationship, but don't try to control it. Deal with and face your own personal fears, your bitterness, your pride, whatever it is that causes you to feel the need to be in control. I can be the priest of my home without feeling like I am dominant. I can have authority without being dogmatic. Come face to face with these things so your marriage can flow. Work so your marriage can be like the waterfall or the band on the stage that everyone is enjoying. The band is simply enjoying the joy of flowing with each other, but those present get to enjoy the product of their groove.

I pray all of you witness or get to experience your union being enjoyed by people around you because of your relationship groove. When you step into a room, there should be such a glow that people enjoy being in your presence. You should enjoy your marriage. You shouldn't dread coming home because things are not going well or because you fear tonight will be the night it all falls apart. Allow the Holy Spirit to lead, guide, and heal so you can mirror the relationship of the Trinity with consistent flow: love, harmony, trust, generosity, kindness, and encouragement for each other.

YOUR TURN

In what ways are you attempting to control your relationship? Why?

_____

_____

_____

_____

How has the way you saw communication throughout your childhood affected how you communicate in your relationship?

_____

_____

_____

Within the chapter Jonathan mentions self-care as a way of taking care of himself within marriage. How are you and your significant other prioritizing self-care and self-awareness to keep your relationship healthy?

_____

_____

_____

I QUIT LIVING IN THE PAST

"Forgetting the past and looking forward to what lies ahead, I press on to reach the end of the race and receive the heavenly prize for which God, through Christ Jesus, is calling us."

—Philippians 3:13-14

My wife and I met as teenagers—unhealthy teenagers. She was hurt and had been abandoned by her father. I was hurt even though I lived in a home with both my parents. We thought we were each other's rescuers from our childhood traumas, but neither of us knew how to do that because we were both still covered in wounds. So, we did what was easiest and caused the most immediate relief: we got married. But we did not realize that relief was superficial.

No matter how hard I tried, I wasn't winning her heart. I was allowing my fear of losing her to cause me to push her away. I had fears of her not being with me. I was living in the past but worried about the future. I was trying to make things as they had been in a particular season of our marriage—the way they were when we were young and dating. I wanted the reactions and the responses I had gotten then, and I wanted to feel that connection again. I wanted her to be happy like she was when we were young. I didn't realize that by trying to reenact the past and secure my future, I was robbing myself of my now. I was not focused or in tune with where my wife was currently. Instead, I was trapped in the past and seduced by the misty possibilities of what might be.

For years I struggled with anxiety and didn't know it. Instead of living in the now, I was living captive to our past. I was handicapped by my own thoughts and the words of other people. The comments of my family and some of my friends would replay in my mind: *Boy, I hope you know what you're doing; I hope you know what you're getting into; She's not the one for you.* I was so worried about the negative possibilities of our future that I failed to live in and enjoy the now. This caused me to unintentionally create the very thing I was trying to avoid. Fear caused me to avoid the present. I was afraid of where things would go, so I kept trying to control it. I didn't want to lose power, status, or influence.

I had to come to the realization that we are a team of two, and the best way for me to control our relationship is for me to learn to control my own thoughts and actions.

Even before I had a complete understanding of why I did the things I was doing, I began going to therapy to help me deal with myself. However, I couldn't wait

until that was complete to working on controlling my thoughts and actions. I had to put my focus back on being my wife's best friend, loving her in ways that speak to her, and loving her for who she is. She was not my friend's wife, nor was she the guy at church's wife, and I had to stop comparing her to them and trying to convert her to be like them. I intentionally decreased my negative behavior and increased the positive. Part of that was accepting and loving my wife for who she is and taking responsibility for my issues, challenges, and personal growth.

YOUR TURN

How well do you study your spouse?
Note how easy or difficult it is for you to answer the
following questions.

What's the first thing your spouse does when he/she
arrives home after work or extended time away?

_____

_____

_____

What's your spouse's morning routine?

_____

_____

_____

What are three of your spouse's dislikes?

_____

_____

_____

What is your spouse's favorite color? _____

List three noticeable changes that have taken place with your spouse since the time you met your spouse until now. Share these with your spouse.

_____

_____

_____

I QUIT TRYING TO BE THE PROVIDER

"And this same God who takes care of me will supply all of your needs from His glorious riches, which have been given to us in Christ Jesus."

—Philippians 4:19 (NLT)

Throughout my journey as a husband and a father, I have learned I am not the source but a resource, a vessel that God uses to get the provision to the house. It's not all up to me.

Growing up, I was always taught the man was to be the provider for the house. The man has to make sure the bills are paid, and the money he made was available to help meet the needs of the household such as bills, food, everyday operations, health care, a car, etc. The man was to be the breadwinner, and the woman was to

take care of the home (even if she worked). I saw my dad do this as I grew up. He worked hard to provide for his family: my mom, my two older brothers, my sister, and me. He had all the answers, and he knew how to get things done.

My dad was very strong. His physical body was that of a powerful man. He stood tall, about six foot four, and had a full build. His character was even stronger. In fact, I remember the first and only time I saw my dad break down where he seemed to be hurt and even cried. He had worked on a particular job for over twenty years, which had been all of my life and then some. The plant wasn't far from our house, and he had worked there over time, moving up in leadership in the company. One day, the company made some cutbacks. They began laying people off, starting with leadership. My dad was a supervisor, and I remember the day he got the news. He came home, sat us all down, and told us he had lost his job. He started to cry and said, "I don't know how I am going to take care of y'all." I saw my dad weep. Seeing him cry did something to us. It did something to *me*. Until this point, I had never seen my dad like that before. I had never seen him cry, and I had to be at least fourteen years old at this particular time. My dad was a strong man. Nothing made him cry except the uncertainty of how he would take care of us. If the only thing to make such a strong man cry was the care of his family, then that was a very serious responsibility and task.

That left a mark on me about the importance of taking care of your family. It left a mark on me as it related to my dad. All my life I had only seen him one way: strong. Now, to see him broken was difficult and hard for me to understand.

Seeing him like that was kind of like when the disciples saw Jesus in the book of Mark. The first eight chapters of Mark present Jesus as the mighty Messiah. He's performing miracles, walking on water, casting out demons, and healing people, and He's really bossing. He's showing that He is powerful, mighty, and in charge. In the eighth chapter, however, around the twenty-seventh verse, Jesus has a conversation with His disciples:

> "Who do people say that I am?" And they told him, "John the Baptist, and others say, Elijah; and others, one of the prophets." And he asked them, "But who do you say that I am?" Peter answered him, "You are the Christ." And He strictly charged them to tell no one about him.

> —Mark 8:27-30, ESV

Jesus went on to modify what Peter said. He was in fact the Savior, but he would have to suffer. "And he began to teach them that the Son of Man must suffer many things and be rejected by the elders and the chief priests and the scribes and be killed, and after three days rise again" (Mark 8:31-32, ESV). He said it plainly in those verses, and from that point on in the eighth chapter, we see the sufferings of Jesus. I can imagine how the disciples were feeling. They probably were in disbelief. As a matter of fact, the eighth chapter of Mark gives an account of three encounters where Christ had to tell them over and over that he was going to suffer before they finally accepted it. That had to be difficult for the disciples to comprehend—the King was going to have to suffer. In their eyes, Jesus suffering meant he was weak or losing. That's a normal human reaction

to suffering. This was different for them because Jesus had always conquered.

That's exactly how I felt when I saw my dad in that moment of his life. All of my life I saw him in powerful positions. I saw him conquer so much, and then I saw him fall. I saw him in what looked like in failure and weakness. When Jesus suffered, He had to give up and give in to the will of the Father, God. My dad also had to give up. We found out later he had not lost. Losing his job was not his demise nor the destruction of our family. It was not to shame him or embarrass him. God set him up and put him in the place where he was supposed to be so he could accomplish what he was intended to accomplish and do what he was ordained to do. He ended up going into the ministry and pastoring full-time. God even relocated him, something that would not have happened had he remained on that job. Even Jesus's suffering propelled Him toward his destiny: dying on the cross and saving mankind.

It took me a while to understand that revelation. For years, I wanted to be in charge because all the men I watched as I grew up took on and carried the weight of that responsibility—my dad, my uncles, pastors, even coaches, teachers, and leaders in our church. That generation of men (the baby boomers), who were my influencers at the time, believed the man was supposed to be the one to make sure the family was taken care of in all aspects. If the family was not taken care of, it was because of negligence or failure on the part of the husband. Therefore, the man would have to figure out a way to make it work out and fall back into alignment in order for the home to get back on track. We were taught this in church, and I saw it in many of their lives. (Mind you, my dad was my pastor for much of my life.)

This was the behavior that had been modeled to me, so it's the behavior I adopted.

I carried that task, responsibility, and burden into my marriage. It shaped my perception of the husband's role. I was to make sure the needs of my family were met, and I took on the full burden of that responsibility. One of the hardest things for me was to see my family struggle or to even imagine my family struggling financially. One of the most important things for me was to make sure my family's needs were met. I needed to make sure we had food, clothing, a roof over our heads, transportation, and the ability to get some of the things we desired as well.

So, when we got married, I felt like it was my job to make sure the bills were paid, things were taken care of around the house, etc. My wife has always had a good-paying job or a very profitable business. But I still carried within me the burden of providing for the family for no other reason than because I was the man and that was what I should do. If anything went wrong in my house, especially financially, it would be a reflection on me. That burden caused a lot of stress on me and in my marriage.

In actuality, it was never my job or responsibility. I was *not* the provider. God was the provider, and I was only a vessel, the resource for the source (God) to use to provide for me and my family. God is Jehovah Jireh. I had to learn how to step back, take my hands off, and have the faith to allow Him to be precisely that. I had to believe and accept that He desires to take care of me and my family. But like Jesus, I had to die to myself and my way of thinking like my dad had to die (figuratively) to the way he said and did things.

Carrying that load was a kind of suffering for me. I'm not necessarily saying going to work is suffering—we all

need to work or have some means of income. But the load and responsibility of providing, as though I was the actual provider, was a weight. Learning to trust Him to provide was transforming for me. I had to reprogram and completely transform my way of thinking. I had to go through hard times to get the point of release. We've lost houses, and we have lost automobiles. We have had the electricity, gas, and water turned off—not always because we didn't have the money but because so much was going on that I forgot to pay the bill. Those hard times enabled me to release the control I thought I had to have. I got to the point where I wasn't sleeping at night, trying to figure things out. I was edgy, and I was angry because I wanted to make sure everything was working out the way I believed it was supposed to. I was working extra jobs and adding more to my plate instead of allowing God to give me a strategy and open the doors I needed.

When I released the control of having to figure things out my way, I released the title and responsibility of being the provider. By doing this, I made room for *the provider*, Jehovah Jireh, to show up and take over. I was in His way, and it caused us to miss out on so many things God had for us. When I moved out of God's position, my family began to thrive; doors of opportunity swung open. Stress and anxiety were finally released. God's blessings began to manifest in my life, my family, and my home.

YOUR TURN

Finances may not be the area that is causing stress within your marriage, however, there are stressors within every marriage. What is that stress within your relationship?

_____

_____

_____

What are the necessary steps you feel you need to take to resolve this stressor?

_____

_____

_____

I QUIT BEING "BUSY" AND STARTED PAYING ATTENTION

"Stop and smell the roses."

—Walter Hagen

It's very easy to become so engulfed in "doing life" that we forget to pay attention to the details and joys of the life we are living. When you have been in a relationship with the same person since you were thirteen or fourteen years old, the twenty or thirty passing years can make it even easier to become jaded with personal desires and (even more so) personal needs. That was the case for me and my wife.

I worked at a private Christian school and held several positions: campus pastor, fine arts director, and Bible and band teacher. In addition to the weekly chapel and occasional pastoral counseling sessions, I ran my own company, which included traveling as a musician and running a private music academy. To top all of that off, I was in school, studying to receive my degree. You may be wondering, "How in the world?" Yeah, sometimes I look back and ask the same thing.

While running in the rat race of life, I seemingly lost touch with my wife and the things she needed. Time moved on as she evolved and grew, but I didn't grow with her in the same capacity and direction. In doing so, we grew apart emotionally because I missed many of the cues—or *bids*, as researcher John Gottman[4] calls them. According to Gottman, bids are attempts made by a person with the desire or intention of connecting with their partner.

Gottman conducted research to answer this question: what separates relationship masters from relationship disasters? With his colleague Robert Levenson, he conducted research at the University of Washington for over forty years. He brought couples into the "Love Lab," an observation facility, and recorded them (with permission) as they discussed their relationship. After couples were prompted to share how they first met and to tell about their most recent fight, he was able to gather information and make critical observations about the couples' relationships. Some couples spent the week in an apartment equipped with cameras to see how they interacted during the practical moments of their everyday.

The researchers followed up with these couples six years later and were able to divide them into two groups: the masters and the disasters. The masters were the ones

who were still together, happily married. The disasters were the couples who were no longer together or who were together but were not happy.

In his book *The Relationship Cure*[5], John Gottman writes, "but after many months of watching these tapes with students, it dawned on me. Maybe it's not the depth of intimacy in conversations that matters. Maybe it doesn't even matter whether couples agree or disagree. Maybe the important thing is how these people pay attention to each other, no matter what they're talking about or doing." In a nutshell, the successful couples were attentive. They listened to each other, and they put their phones/devices down or turned them off when the other person needed or wanted to chat or simply spend time together.

From this research, Gottman developed the philosophy for building healthy relationships: healthy couples constantly make and accept bids to connect. Gottman defines bids as "the fundamental unit of emotional communication." Bids can be verbal or nonverbal. They can be big or small. They are simple requests from one partner to connect to the other. Bids can be an expression or statement, a question, or even a simple touch. They can be serious or funny, general or even sexual. Bids simply invite and request the other person to connect with you on various levels. A bid is anything you do that allows your partner or spouse to respond.

For example, your partner may ask, "What did your supervisor ever say about the request you submitted?" or "Did you ever get a chance to call your sister back? What did she want?" They may ask, "Do you still want to go to the movies this weekend?" or simply "Can you pass the remote?" They can give you a quick wink, brush up against you and reach for your hand, or give you a tight hug. All of these are bids regardless of how

subtle they may appear to be. A bid usually means "I want your attention; I need to feel connected to you." Both husbands and wives give bids at some point in their marriage.

There are three ways to respond to a bid: turn towards (acknowledge the bid), turn away (ignore or miss the bid), and turn against (reject the bid in an argumentative or belligerent way). If your spouse lets out a sigh while looking through text messages, that's a bid. In an effort to turn towards them, you would simply ask, "What's wrong?" or "Is everything okay?" A grunt or even totally ignoring the sigh and doing nothing, however, would be turning away from your spouse. Posing an attack against your spouse such as, "What's wrong with you now? You always have something going on. Don't you see I'm trying to read?" Those are all ways to turn against your partner's bid.

I remember trying to connect with my wife by buying her a pair of nice earrings. She had passively mentioned wanting another pair of gold hoop earrings, so one day, unbeknownst to her I went to the mall and bought her a pair of fourteen-karat gold hoop earrings. I put the jewelry bag and box on her pillow so she would be sure to see it when she got home. She looked at them, sat them on the nightstand, and proceeded with her evening. I had been so sure I would get a different response, and here's why I didn't.

It wasn't that my wife was ungrateful; she did say thank you. It was because the big gestures mean less when there is no true emotional connection. Now, she could have given me the superficial response I wanted— she is a great actress—but that would not have been genuine or authentic. It's not the gifts that make relationships but the acceptance of bids that does it. If I had not reached out to her all day, if I hadn't paid attention

to her bid when she walked in the door, the jewelry box was not going to substitute for that. If I had not been paying attention all week, a big gesture on Friday was not going to cover up for it.

Gottman suggests relationships be built and maintained with daily attention, not grand gestures. No, we are not going to accept all of our spouses' bids. However, masters tend to accept more than disasters do. He points out how relationships can't be placed on ice for a while and then thawed out with a fancy gift or classy dinner. Couples should bid often. The good thing is bids can be short and simple, but they go a long way. The goal is to make and accept as many bids in a day's time as you can with your spouse. Gottman observed masters bid one hundred times at the dinner table in a short ten-minute time span. The disasters only bid sixty-five times in the same time frame.

Giving and accepting bids shows your spouse your desire to connect. As a matter of fact, the happiest and healthiest couples bid all the time. It can be a note on the bathroom mirror, an "I know you can do it!" text right before an important presentation, or even a six-second kiss when your spouse walks in the door. (Gottman suggests all kisses last a minimum of six seconds.) When my wife's bids were ignored, she began to hold onto the negative emotions attached to them. Her brain subconsciously was keeping a tally of the number of bids she gave, the number of bids I accepted, and how many times I turned away from or ignored them. She became more and more upset and resentful when I turned away from and against her bids. They turned into arguments, more shutdowns, and more bitterness. She was feeling angry and betrayed. We began to be more and more disconnected.

When I finally slowed down and started paying attention, I was able to see and understand my wife's bids. When I started turning towards those bids, my wife felt valued, cared for, and appreciated. It built trust in our relationship, and that snowballed into more passion for each other, more emotional connection, and a better, more satisfying sex life. Slow down. Tomorrow will take care of itself. Pay attention to what's going on around you. It can and will make a difference in your relationships.

YOUR TURN

Take some time to evaluate areas in your life that you may be missing because of "busy-ness."

Would you currently label your relationship a master or disaster? Why or why not?

_____

_____

_____

How can you become more intune with your spouse's needs and desires?

_____

_____

_____

Take some time to identify bids that you and your significant other have put out in the last 7-14 . How have you both responded to each other's bids?

_____

_____

_____

How could you approach them and respond better?

_____

_____

_____

I QUIT COACHING AND STARTED HAVING CONVERSATIONS

"Most people don't listen with the intent to understand, most people listen with the intent to reply."

—Stephen R. Covey

Women often get frustrated with men because they don't see things the same way or because they hear things differently. Vice versa, men get upset with their wives because they don't feel like they hear them. That's where I was. I would try to explain something to my wife or communicate with her, and it was as if she wasn't hearing what I was saying. Her interpretation of what I was saying would be totally different from what I

thought I was saying. I would become very frustrated with her when this would happen because I didn't have this problem with all women. I worked with a team of women from all over the world at my job. I communicated with these women on a regular basis. When I had staff meetings with them, they understood me. I let them know their roles, what we were going to do as a team, and how God was going to bless us in what we were doing. They would leave the meeting excited, uplifted, and encouraged. Even when I had to get firm with them, they understood, and they still respected me and my authority.

I would come home, and I would try to share my vision with my wife, and she simply didn't hear me and couldn't see it. Sometimes it was the timing in which I would say things, and sometimes the enemy (the devil) distorted what I was trying to say. Then I thought, *It may be spiritual.* The enemy had to have us blinded, I thought.

Over time I realized home was different from work. My work team and home team were different and couldn't be approached in quite the same way. Our roles and responsibilities were distinctively different. Not only that, but I also had to take a look at the timing of our conversations. I had to realize I needed to code-switch. Code-switching is how you speak based on the context of the environment. There is a code for the athletic field/team and one for your staff, a code for the teacher, and a code for the preacher. Then, there is a code for the father and the husband all based on the context of the environment in which he is speaking and the situation that is being addressed or discussed. This is true not simply for the husband but literally with everyone.

I am by nature a very energetic and animated person. I love to motivate and encourage people to do and become better. In essence, I'm a coach. In the past, I was actually a track coach for a community track club, and I absolutely loved it! When I was younger, I thought one day I would be a basketball coach. When I think about it, I was accustomed to coaching. I coached my team at work and in the classroom. I would teach or coach my students into purpose and to have the passion to pursue their dreams. I used a certain energy and tone when I was coaching. When I came home and presented something to my wife, I would often still be in "coach" mode. I had to learn to turn the coach, teacher, and pastor off. My wife needed me to be a husband and friend more than she needed me to be her coach. I had to learn to let communication happen authentically and organically without having to be so official in our conversations. I learned how she hears me best, and I listened to her when she told me things and when she dropped hints. It wasn't the message that needed to be changed so much as it was the delivery and the voice used to communicate the message.

We learned and mastered how to control conversations, which assured they didn't spiral into an argument. We began using reflective conversation. To reflect means to take a look at something deeply or think about something. In a reflective conversation, both parties listen and think about what is being said. In the beginning it was difficult, and we thought it would not be a natural way to have a conversation. Once we practiced it, however, it became an authentic and effective way to communicate. This technique of communication was centered around how we responded (not necessarily how we talked) to each other. It grounded our conversations, and it made our communication productive and healthy.

It wasn't so much that we merely talked to each other, but we communicated with each other with clarity and complete understanding of the topic at hand. We made sure our responses were not judgmental; we didn't place blame, accuse, insult, put down, threaten, call names, or swear. (We don't do that last one anyway.) Even when we disagreed, no one took it personally as an attack from the other party.

Statistics show that in healthy and stable marriages, couples respond to each other eighty percent of the time. When we look at marriages that end in divorce, those couples responded to each other less than fifty percent of the time.

I still wanted to feel heard, and I wanted to feel like my wife got me or understood what I was saying. My wife needed that as well. So, we started mirroring our conversations with each other. (To learn more about this, visit: www.vow2cherish.com and take the free five-day Marriage Masterpiece Challenge.) This technique and style of conversation not only helped us instantly stop arguing, but it helped us to connect to each other in a way that had been broken. Nothing makes you feel more valued and heard than clarity and proper response. The tension disappeared, and our relationship ascended to higher levels of intimacy and love than we had previously known. Our communication grew from merely "talking" to each other to being heard and understood.

YOUR TURN

What do you like most about how you and your spouse communicate, especially when you don't agree?

_____

_____

_____

What do you like least about how you and your spouse communicate, especially when you don't agree?

_____

_____

_____

How can you and your spouse make communication better and make sure both sides are heard?

_____

_____

_____

I QUIT TAKING LIFE
FOR GRANTED

*"Because of the LORD's great love, we are not consumed,
for his compassions never fail.
They are new every morning great is your faithfulness."*

—Lamentations 3:22-23

There are twenty-four hours in one day. That's 1,440 minutes, which is 86,400 seconds in each day. Everybody is given the same amount of time. What we do with that time is quite different from person to person. We have the opportunity to make the most of every second. Once that time is gone, even a second of it, you never get it back. You may get another opportunity, but you can never get *that* particular moment back. When we are living life, it's easy to think we have it figured out. We set our routines. We have our schedules and agendas.

We have our plans. But all of that can change in the blink of an eye—literally.

My wife is the most precious thing to me, but there was a time when I didn't let her know that. I mean, we were on good terms, things were going well, and we were functioning, even thriving—or so I thought. She was telling me I was missing this and overlooking that. I heard her, but I didn't know how she could think in such a way. In my eyes, we were good. I didn't understand why she felt unappreciated and overwhelmed. I was doing what I was doing. Wasn't that enough? But she was tired all the time and didn't seem happy. HHow did I miss it? I was trying to cater to her, but it wasn't enough.

Then it happened. It was a Monday afternoon. We were planning family time at the movies, but she was extremely tired and had a headache. She decided to sleep in and didn't want to get out of bed. I convinced her that a hot shower and time in the sauna would help her feel better, but it didn't. "I think I need something to eat," she said. So, I ordered her favorite hibachi for takeout. As she was telling me her order—teriyaki salmon with fried rice, no egg, fresh ginger and wasabi, two yum-yum sauces, and a side of low sodium soy sauce—her speech became slurred and jumbled. I tried to get her to repeat herself, but it was still slurred. Within seconds she was unconscious. She wasn't out long before she came to. She still complained about not feeling well. She didn't seem to realize what had happened and said she wanted a nap, so I let her rest for about an hour.

She woke up and said she felt well enough to go to the movies, so we did. Long story short, she ended up in the ER the following day for a stroke workup. The doctors were certain she had had a TIA (or mini-istroke). For weeks she dealt with headaches, seizures,

and muscle weakness. She struggled to walk and had a variety of other symptoms. The next few months were filled with neurologists, cardiologists, hospital visits, hospital stays, CT scans, MRIs, spinal taps, and more medication than we even want to talk about. (Ayanna practiced natural health, so she didn't take medication for ailments and symptoms before this.) She was always the one to visit and sit with family and friends while they healed and got better. My wife, the one who only went to the doctor for routine check-ups, the one who had only been admitted into the hospital to deliver our three children, was now the patient herself.

Three months after being out of work on FMLA (Family/Medical Leave), she returned to her job about thirty miles away from our home. Over the course of this time, she was still having seizures. One particular night, after we had returned from meeting my oldest daughter at the airport, she had her most intense seizure up to this point. On a regular day, when she had a seizure, they would totally wipe her out physically, and she would usually sleep for hours after they passed. This night was no different. When it passed, I made sure she took the medicine and helped her to bed. The following morning, though she didn't feel well, she wanted to go to work because she had only recently returned. I urged her to take the day off, but she insisted. (If you know Yanna personally, you understand this battle.) The last thing I wanted to do was cause her to get upset. So, if she was going to go to work, I was going to drive her. (For medical purposes, she wasn't supposed to drive for six months after having a seizure anyway.) The seizure medication she took would make her very groggy, so she literally slept the entire drive.

It was early morning—the weather was dreary, rainy, and dark. While en route, only a few feet from our exit

on the interstate, we were sideswiped by a garbage truck. The truck drug our car several yards up the highway before I was able to disconnect from it. Her car was totaled, but we walked away unharmed.

It was in that moment—hearing the crashing metal, feeling the jolt of the impact, and not knowing what was happening or what the outcome would be—that suddenly I knew what mattered most. Our kids could have lost both parents that morning. I could have lost my wife. (The impact was on the passenger's side.) In that moment, work was not important—she didn't end up going anyway. In that instant, meetings or events didn't cross my mind. The only important thing was that we were okay and everyone was alive. Yanna was alive and unharmed. In the blink of an eye, life could have changed so drastically. Change it did bring but without injury or death. I changed my perspective and started appreciating my life again. We lost the car, but it was soon replaced. We were blessed with life, and that is absolutely irreplaceable!

When I sat back and thought about it, up to this point I would find myself always on the go. I was always in a rush—always "busy." My schedule was packed full—working until three every afternoon, music lessons until five every evening, and taking care of exchange students through the evening as well. I'd come home, cook dinner, and then do homework. (Yeah, I was working on my master's degree online at the time.) There were meetings after school and services and events at church, or perhaps the car needed to go for maintenance. I'd pick up that child there or take this child here. There was always something to do. It seemed like everything was due yesterday. I had to slow down. I had to look at and appreciate the people around me. I had to learn to make the most of every day—each hour, minute,

and second—because tomorrow is not promised to us. Neither is an hour from now, a minute from now, or even a second for now. Don't waste time on something that won't matter in the long run. Cherish the people and things in your life that truly matter.

Walking through my wife's health challenges with her taught me a big lesson. People called, came over, brought meals, prayed, etc., and we were grateful. But when the sun went down and the doors closed, when the visitors left and the conversations ended, it was only me and the kids. We were the ones (though sometimes she would try to hide it from the kids) who saw her unable to walk, unable to hold a bottle, unable to open a soda. It was the people I cherished who were with me; it was the people who really matter that were there. The people I had once taken for granted, that's who I saw when I looked around, and I was so glad we were all there.

Wherever you are in your marriage and relationship, learn to cherish each other. Make the choice to *quit* but not to only quit but *fight as well!* Don't fight each other; fight the urge to give up and walk away. Don't take life for granted. Don't take your spouse or your marriage for granted. You can win. There is hope for you and your marriage is necessary.

YOUR TURN

Take some time to write out the things you admire and cherish about your significant other and your family.

_____

_____

_____

Leave the note in a place where they can find it and let them know that you appreciate & cherish them!

TOGETHER AT LAST

THEOLOGY OF MARRIAGE

"Marriage should be honored by all. . ."

—Hebrews 13:4 (NIV)

God is the architect and creator of marriage, and it's the creator who determines the form and function of his/her creation. You cannot determine what your spouse does. Only God can do that. Marriage is God's gift. It is our belief that marriage can only truly be understood when a person believes in creationism. We are able to experience and enjoy God's gift of marriage and His design for companionship, joy, and ultimately family. We are God's creations and we were created and intended to function and thrive in relationships with others. Before sin entered the world, God decided relationships were important and essential. He established that there would be one earthly relationship that had greater value than the rest: the relationship between husband and wife. Marriage is a very unique relationship and covenant.

It's both a sacred and public promise that bonds two individuals together in a relationship of love, support, nurture, and care. Marriage would be the earthly example, and the only relationship greater would be that of the marriage between Christ and the church.

The marriage covenant reveals the fullness of God's relationship of love, support, and nurture to the world. God's incarnational love is revealed through the life, death, burial, resurrection, and ascension of Jesus Christ. The Holy Spirit gives witness to Jesus and God's unending love through our relationships with one another. Marriage is part of that relational witness to the love that God embodies. That is, those who are united in marriage are called and blessed to give witness and testimony of God's love through the grace of Jesus Christ. This ultimately happens when the relationship is fulfilled through sorrow and joy, plenty and need, sickness and health, offense and reconciliation, living and dying. This vulnerable, loving, intimate relationship and institution of marriage is truly a blessed gift from God.

Why man? Well, man was created for two purposes, to serve and to preserve what God created. According to Genesis 2:15, he was created to preserve: "So the Lord God took the man [He had made] and settled him in the Garden of Eden to cultivate and keep it." And in accordance with Matthew 20:27, he was created to serve: "and whoever wishes to be first among you shall be your [willing and humble] slave."

Why woman? It's in the DNA of creation for women to be counselors. God made women to give perspective to men. Women were created for two purposes: to commune with and to counsel (help) what God has created. Woman are blessed and favored of God (Proverbs 31:10-12 ESV).

When God brought men and women together, He intended for them to bring life through marriage. Marriage was created to be like a river and not a flood. God created the river to bring life to everything it touches. When you look at a river or listen to it, the flow is constant, but it is calm and mellow and can be very serene to observe. A river may have rocks that cause it to get bumpy, but the momentum causes it to maintain constant flow over those bumps. A flood, on the other hand, is a gush. It also flows, but it destroys anything in its path. It's not structured down an orchestrated course like a river. A flood has no boundaries, and it has no limits in its destruction. The more strength and momentum given to a flood; the more destruction occurs. So, a river is created to give life, but if it swells and floods, it goes beyond what it was created to do.

When marriage stays within the limits of what it was created to do, it also gives life. But if it goes outside of those parameters (an example would be extramarital affairs or simply enough disobedience), it destroys. Hence sin entered into the world when the first marriage got outside the boundaries of what it was created for.

So, take a look at your marriage, we had to take the hard look at ours. Not the marriage that was on display for others to see, but the marriage that operated daily behind closed doors. We had to ask ourselves the hard question: *is our marriage honorable*? Is God getting total and consistent honor out of our marriage? Is our marriage honoring God both publicly and privately? We encourage you to do the same. Any part of your marriage, public or private, that is not honorable should be changed. Cherish the gift that God has given, the gift of marriage.

YOUR TURN

Take a look at your marriage/relationship

Do you view your marriage as a gift? Why or why not?

_____

_____

_____

What were the top 5 reasons your wanted to marry your spouse?

_____

_____

_____

_____

Do you consider your marriage (currently) a river or a flood? Why?

_____

_____

_____

How has your marriage gotten outside the boundaries of what it was created for?

_____

_____

_____

_____

_____

What destruction erupted because of that detour?

_____

_____

_____

How can you be aware of and avoid a detrimental course change?

_____

_____

_____

How can boundaries be reestablished in order to put your marriage back on track to being honorable?

_____

_____

_____

WE QUIT USING THE "D" WORD

"Never give up, for that is just the place and time that the tide will turn."

—Harriet Beecher Stowe

Most experts, therapists, counselors, coaches, and even pastors will tell you falling in love is the easy part of a marriage. They will usually also tell you that staying in love is the hard part. Most married couples will agree that maintaining a thriving, healthy, and successful marriage is demanding and takes hard work and effort on both sides. For some, staying married may be very difficult. Many of us want to live happily ever after with the same person but sometimes find it to be an arduous task.

No matter how much you love your spouse, no matter how happy you are, one thing is certain. You will experience conflict at some point in your marriage. You will disagree, and you may even argue and fight. Conflict in any relationship is inevitable. How you respond to the conflict, however, is another subject.

When we first married, we were stressed, overwhelmed, and unsure. We had to handle new choices, new systems, unfamiliar conflicts, and all of our differences. The problem was we didn't know how to handle those differences or our disagreements. We didn't understand how to solve our problems in a healthy way that would actually preserve and protect the love we genuinely felt for each other. We were on the verge of destroying our marriage because we had destructive fighting habits. Almost every big argument or fight we had would end in the use of the "D" word: divorce. But how? Jonathan was my best friend. And why? Ayanna was the absolute best thing to happen to me.

We met and were attracted to each other. We shared dates and laughs. We went to movies, picnics in parks, museums, and every fine restaurant in Atlanta. We fell in love. There was excitement, and there was heat. But then we got married. Problems came, and we stopped going to the movies. We stopped having picnics in the park, visiting museums, and eating out. We had less fun. We stopped talking and treating each other like friends. We started looking at each other and seeing stress. We started associating those feelings with pain rather than the fun and support we once knew. This put our marriage at risk. Ayanna was the product of a broken home, so divorce was always an option for her. When we had heated discussions, there would always be an escape plan in the rafters. But why?

We were allowing the main causes of divorce to enter our marriage, and they were taking over. John Gottman[2] refers to them as the Four Horsemen, and ninety percent of marriages where the Horsemen are present are at risk of divorce. Though most relationships will see and experience the presence of these Horsemen at some point or other, it's the healthy relationships that rarely experience this. So, what are the Four Horsemen?

Criticism is the first. Criticism is defined here as making disapproving judgments or evaluations about your spouse. In simpler terms, it is pretty much letting your spouse know that something is wrong with them and that it needs to be fixed. Phrases that begin, "You always . . ." or "You never . . ." are examples. This Horseman is good for attacking your spouse's character. How do you dismantle this Horseman? You talk about your feelings by using "I" statements, then express a positive need. You can then express yourself, even complain, without blaming and without using generalizations.

Contempt is the second Horseman. Contempt is the act of perceiving inferiority or undesirability and can include name-calling, eye-rolling, sneering, cynicism, showing disgust, or mockery. If your statement seems to place you higher and your spouse lower, that's contempt. Experts use the presence of contempt as a predictor of relationship failure. How did we overcome contempt? We treated each other with respect and began to show genuine, authentic appreciation for each other. (Our *Love Notes Journal* helped with this and is available at www.Vow2Cherish.com).

The third Horseman is defensiveness. You are being defensive if you are defending yourself against a presumed attack instead of listening. It's having your guard up just in case. This causes each of us at some point to play the victim, responding to what we see as an

attack and counteracting it with a complaint or mutual criticism. How did we get rid of this one? We began to truly hear what the other was actually saying (especially complaints) without taking it personally. Then, we began to accept responsibility for the problem. (See Ayanna's chapter: "I Quit Playing the Blame Game.")

The final Horseman is stonewalling. It's refusing to listen to your spouse, particularly his/her complaints. You either physically or mentally withdraw yourself from the conversation. You shut down and stop paying attention. This can become a habit. What can make this even worse is if the other person tries to force a conversation or solution attempt after the first person stonewalls. Stonewalling is usually a response, or a subsidiary of the negativity and tension created by the first three Horsemen. Why do people stonewall? There are many reasons.

One reason is belligerence: being provocative and challenging your spouse's power and authority. People who use this tactic are usually looking for a fight. What's the solution? Couples should have a plan in place to take a twenty-minute break away from each other and then come back to the conversation after that twenty minutes has expired.

When we married, we were both young, hurting, and very unhealthy emotionally. But it didn't appear to be that way on the surface. We were both smart and very mature. Though we didn't have shouting and yelling matches often, and we never resorted to phys-ical violence, our arguments would escalate in subtler ways. We would return negative comments for negative comments. We would point fingers and say some cruel things—things we honestly didn't mean or feel but knew would hurt. During an escalating fight or argument, the main objective is to purposely hurt your spouse with

your words. But once those words are spoken, there's no way to take them back. You can ask your spouse for forgiveness, and they may eventually be able to forgive you. But, of course, it would be better not to have said it. Looking back, if we had not been as stressed, tired, and frustrated as we were, if we hadn't both been so vocal, we could have heard each other more and hurt each other less. Even in conversations where we were not intentionally crass and hateful, there were things said that could be categorized as insensitive, which left one or the other feeling disrespected. Whenever words leave your spouse feeling as though their thoughts, feelings, or opinions are wrong or unimportant, it can be very harmful to the marriage. More often than not, it makes the person being put down feel as though what they have to say is insignificant, and it may cause them to internalize their feelings rather than say what they genuinely think.

We found that a lot of the time, what we had thought was the source of our issues really wasn't. There were often hidden problems at the core. There were unspoken expectations, buried needs, hidden fears, and suppressed feelings that caused a lot of frustration. We had to identify those hidden issues so they could no longer threaten our relationship.

We had to learn how to show respect for each other, especially when we had to talk about sensitive topics. We had to set rules for our talks: 1) use "I" statements, 2) no interruptions, and 3) summarize what you heard before responding. At first, it didn't seem like it would be very natural, but it worked. The more we used this method of communicating, the more natural it became.

After working through our issues and getting to the core of what was really going on, we were eventually able to make the decision that we were in it for the

long haul. We realized we were better together, even if we went through times of frustration, anger, and even misunderstanding. We are a team, and teams have issues and encounter conflict. But they don't let that stop them. Teams don't win every game, but they keep showing up for practice. They look at the films from the last game, sort out the mistakes, and point out the good plays. They study the strategies and plays of the opposing team. With all of that information in hand, they make a plan for their next game. We took timeouts when necessary, but no one was going anywhere, and *divorce* was not ever going to be an option for us again. We stopped using the word, and the fear of someone leaving stopped paralyzing the growth of our relationship. A conversation, a decision, and a plan took the word out of our vocabulary for good. We don't even play with the idea in a joking manner.

Of course, people don't usually marry with the intention to divorce. However, in the society we live in, divorce is widely accepted and in some cases suggested or even recommended. For years, statistics showed the divorce rate in the United States was a whopping fifty percent. The CDC[3] shows that rate has decreased significantly. However, the decrease in divorce is likely correlated to the decrease in the number of marriages taking place, making it difficult to achieve an accurate percentage. The takeaway from this statistic is that not as many couples are divorcing, at least in America, because not as many are getting married as before.

Through strategy and wisdom, God taught us to be good stewards of our marriage because someday we will have to give an account to God for that stewardship. As couples, we have to do our part regardless of what the other does, what they say, or how they act. We have to each be accountable. We can't negotiate this

with our spouse because it's a mandate from God. We wanted the marriage that God designed for us to have. We had to see our marriage through the eyes of God in order to have that. We had to remind ourselves of Mark 10:9 (AMP), which says, "Therefore, what God has united *and* joined together, man must not separate [by divorce]". That includes us.

Pray God shows you any wrong thoughts, motives, and actions you have as it relates to your spouse and marriage so He can help you steward what He has given you. Redefine your perspective and allow yourself to shift from *I quit* to *I refuse to quit*. Find ways to rekindle the fire, restore the love, and reinvent your marriage.

Even when walking away seems rights, allow your marriage to be saved!

YOUR TURN

In what ways do you steward your marriage or relationship?

_____

_____

_____

How can you improve the stewardship of your marriage or relationship?

_____

_____

_____

Which Horsemen have been present throughout the duration of your marriage?

_____

_____

_____

If any are still present, what will you do to get rid of it/them?

_____

_____

_____

WE MEET IN THE MIDDLE

"The area of your deepest wound will be the area of your greatest impact."

—Unknown

Y ou may be wondering about the title of this section of the book and this chapter. *Together at last? We meet in the middle?* We get it. We met and have been together since the introduction of the book when you read through *Our Story.* But also, as you've read, there was more to being together than just being a couple and married, we had to be on the same page, the same frequency, the same heartbeat. We didn't start out that way.

One thing about Jonathan and me is that we rarely shared the full details of what was going on in our marriage with other people. We got married young and kept our marriage a secret for nine full months. In essence, the foundation of our marriage was secrecy and deceit. We knew how to hide, how to cover up, and how to

position the mask ever so perfectly so no one could see behind it (yes that created and cultivated negative culture in our relationship). We would tell our best friends, our therapists/counselors, and even our pastors the truth about certain details, but that was pretty much it, and even that was limited. I would only tell so much about Jonathan because I wanted to protect his reputation with people. Jonathan would tell some things about me and limit information about himself. But the bottom line, we eventually needed more and that was not going to happen until we really opened the box and dealt with the root of issues that surfaced. Contrary to the ideals we had held on to for a while, my husband was not the root cause of my issues. Neither was I the cause of his issues. Even though it was disguised as such and caused us to often lash out against each other, maturity gave us a different perspective.

We made the conscious decision to quit fighting each other and started fighting to win in our marriage as a team. We realized we were not each other's enemy. We were on the same team, fighting for the same finished product. We had the same goal. We recognized who our opponent was and focused all of our energy and efforts on destroying what was hurting us. We had to destroy the pain. We began fighting the real sources of the problem: generational iniquity (sin), generational curses/cycles, generational mindsets, and word curses from others outside our home as well as from ourselves. We launched an attack back three generational dimensions. In psychology it is known and believed that the actions and behaviors as far as three generations back can still affect a child (or in our case, adult) in the present day. We increased our prayers, increased our prayer time together, and we received professional counseling both as individuals and as a couple. We changed our

perspective on our marriage and each other. It took time. It didn't happen over night. But when changed, we began to win, and our relationship was restored. Our love was reignited. I found the friend with whom I loved spending time and with whom I loved to talk. I found the one I cared for and who cared for me. I found the one I fell in love with as a teenager. I found the friend that I talked to on the phone until the wee hours of the morning. Yes, I found my friend. And my husband found his.

So, what caused the problem or disconnection? Our vision had gotten distorted over time, and life had caused those distortions. We weren't able to identify any major event; we simply didn't want to be bothered with each other anymore. Life, jobs, children, church, family, businesses, obligations, habits, and general busy-ness was causing us to slowly, subtly drift apart. When we looked up, we were on two separate parts of the sea of life and didn't even realize how much distance was now between us. Life forced us to make a decision, and we decided we were on the same team and wanted the same thing. We wanted the love and relationship that was planned for us in the beginning, and we fought and quit to make it happen.

Once we were healed and our marriage began to blossom and grow, people would try to encourage us to tell our story, but we weren't interested. It was enough for us and our marriage to be healed; we weren't doing it for anybody else. Besides, we didn't want the judgment of people who thought they knew us but never really *knew* us. We didn't want people to see our failures or our scars. One night after an emergency marriage intervention session with our marriage mentors, one of them looked at us and said, "It's time for you to tell your story. The world needs to hear it."

It was then we realized why we had gone through what we had in our marriage. We had to realize our journey, our story had absolutely nothing to do with us. When we thought it wasn't even worth telling, we had to realize it was what other couples needed to hear. We grew in understanding of what marriage is. (It was not simply a legal avenue to have sex) We received the revelation that marriage is the beginning of a generation and a bloodline. Marriage was the very first covenant created. Indeed, marriage is the first relationship in the Bible we get to see, and it is near and dear to the heart of God. The intentional attack on our marriage and all marriages is the intent to destroy the family. To destroy bloodlines. To destroy generations. We had to fight for our marriage. We had to fight for our bloodline. We had to fight for the generations that will come behind us. We had to fight for our marriage to help save yours.

If we had to endure all we went through to save even one marriage, then it was all worth it. If I had to go through all of this to save my bloodline, it was worth it. We had to save the next generation. We had to save a lineage. We had to destroy the curse of divorce. We had to destroy the curse of toxic marriage and restore healthy, whole marriage to our bloodline so our children, their children, and generations to follow could have healthy and wholesome marriages. We had seen enough divorce. We had seen enough couples staying together but really being separate. We had seen enough of simply "being together" to save face but being secretly miserable. We quit hiding behind our pain and decided to use it to help other people.

It was for you—the engaged couple. You can quit now before you even get married. The best way to prepare for marriage is to identify and quit those toxic habits and actions that can be detrimental to your long-lasting and

healthy marriage. It was for the newly married couple that has fears of what will happen because of a marriage model they have seen in the past. It was for you, the couple that is tired and ready to throw in the towel. It can get better. It was for you, the couple that feels like something is missing and that no matter what you try, you don't seem to click anymore. Take a look at what wasn't working for us, evaluate the root of what's not working for you, and *quit*! It will save your marriage too. If you take a good look at what you can quit and begin to work on those areas, your spouse will in turn do the same. Before you know it, you will be quitting together. You are fighting the same opponent as a team.

Don't worry. It seemed daunting for us in the beginning, too, but now we have grown. We have matured. We know ourselves better. We know each other better. We've learned to cherish the little things because they are often the things that matter most. Do we still have challenges? Of course—we are still human, and new things come up. However, we face each day as a new adventure on the journey of lasting love and marriage, and so will you!

YOUR TURN

List five things you can do today to make your spouse feel more valued, loved, and appreciated.

_____

_____

_____

_____

_____

What stops you from doing those things on a regular basis?

_____

_____

_____

If you don't know of ways to improve your marriage or relationship, let's start first with a good look at each other individually and together as a couple. How do your personalities match?

_____

_____

_____

How do your personalities differ? _____

_____

_____

APPENDECIES

NOTES

1 Gary D. Chapman and Jocelyn Green, *The 5 Love Languages: the Secret to Love That Lasts* (Chicago, IL: Northfield Publishing, 2015).

2 Ellie Lisitsa, "The Gottman Institute ," *The Gottman Institute* (blog), April 23, 2013, https://www.gottman.com/blog/the-four-horsemen-recognizing-criticism-contempt-defensiveness-and-stonewalling/.

3 "NVSS - Marriages and Divorces," Centers for Disease Control and Prevention (Centers for Disease Control and Prevention, January 13, 2017), https://www.cdc.gov/nchs/nvss/marriage-divorce.htm?CDC_AA_refVal=https%3A%2F%2Fwww.cdc.gov%2Fnchs%2Fmardiv.htm.

4 John Mordechai Gottman and Joan DeClaire, *The Relationship Cure: a Five-Step Guide to Strengthening*

Your Marriage, Family, and Friendships (New York, NY: Harmony Books, 2002).

5 John Mordechai Gottman and Joan DeClaire, *The Relationship Cure: a Five-Step Guide to Strengthening Your Marriage, Family, and Friendships* (New York, NY: Harmony Books, 2002), 28.

ACKNOWLEDGEMENTS

To Our Children

We thank God for you. Throughout the course of not only the writing part of this process but the part where we actually had to live it out and actually get to the point of quitting you guys have been there. Thank you for cheering us on and for being a huge part of our *why*. We are better because of you guys and we absolutely love you! #ThatKilgoreKrew

• • •

To Our Parents: Mama Fleet & Mama Kilgore

We don't take all you have done and do for us for granted. We appreciate and love you always.

ABOUT THE AUTHORS

Jonathan & Ayanna Kilgore met as teenagers, became high school sweethearts, and married while in college. They entered marriage with a lot of personal baggage and different perspectives they had to work through. Through their work with Vow2Cherish™ Marriage Network, they mentor and coach couples to prepare engaged couples for the journey ahead, and they equip new and seasoned couples with valuable tools to grow their friendship and relationship with each other. They are not only committed to reminding couples of their vow to love but emphasizing the powerful Vow2Cherish.

Married 24 years, Jonathan & Ayanna have weathered challenges with "growing up while married" and

are now living in their happily ever after. Blessed with three young-adult children, Jadyn, Jemarcus, and Nysi, they continue to complete their fairytale dreams.

Licensed and ordained ministers, certified marriage mentors, and relationship coaches, Jonathan & Ayanna have helped countless couples assess and evaluate their relationship. They do this by creating a strategic roadmap to make their marriages the healthy masterpieces they were created to become. Jonathan & Ayanna speak at marriage conferences, retreats, seminars, and events.
Connect at Vow2Cherish.com

YOU'VE READ *I QUIT,*
Now where do you start?

Evaluate your marriage/relationship and get a
roadmap for your for quitting!

Take the Marriage Assessment
&
Get a Couples Coaching Session
Vow2Cherish.com

Join the Vow2Cherish™ Marriage Network

Today

CLOSE THE GAP BETWEEN
DREAMING & DOING AS A COUPLE

BECOME AN UNHACKABLE COUPLE

Learn More

MyUnhackableMarriage.com

EVERY PURCHASE COUNTS.

THANKS FOR CHANGING LIVES WITH US.

Your purchase has changed a life. We've partnered with B1G1.com to donate to over 500 causes worldwide. You've clothe families, planted trees, dug wells, educated children, rescued women, and so much more.

Your purchase (and future purchases) has helped people around the world in desperate need of life's most basic essentials. Thank you.

**Flip the book now and begin reading
Gentlemen Next**